THE PARK

A GUIDE TO THE
CRAGS & HIGH PEAKS
OF
ROCKY MOUNTAIN
NATIONAL PARK

THE PARK: A Guide to the Crags & High Peaks of Rocky Mountain National Park

ISBN   0-9657079-9-7

Front cover photos: Flying Buttress on Mount Meeker by Steve "Crusher" Bartlett. Photo of Crusher on South Buttress of Notchtop by Fran Bagenal. Content page photo of Gary Neptune on Flying Buttress by Clyde Soles, Neptune collection. Interior photos: Uncredited scenic photos by Mike Stevens. Uncredited action photos by Fred Knapp.

Special thanks to my sister, Daniela Knapp, for her help with maps, topos, and editing
—Fred

WARNING:

Climbing is extremely dangerous and could result in injury or death. Information in this book may be inaccurate as it is based on the authors' impressions and memories as well as information from other sources. The condition of rock and fixed gear can change dramatically in an alpine environment. Assume responsibility for your own actions and decisions; use good judgement; and be prepared to retreat at any expense. Have fun but be safe.

IMAGE FROM A PHOTO BY CRAIG DILLON

Black Diamond

ROCK CLIMBING   ICE CLIMBING
BACKCOUNTRY SKIING   ALPINISM

2084 EAST 3900 SOUTH
SALT LAKE CITY, UT 84124
CONTACT US FOR A FREE
C A T A L O G
PHONE: (801) 278-5533
E-MAIL: climb@bdel.com
BlackDiamondEquipment.com

Table of Contents

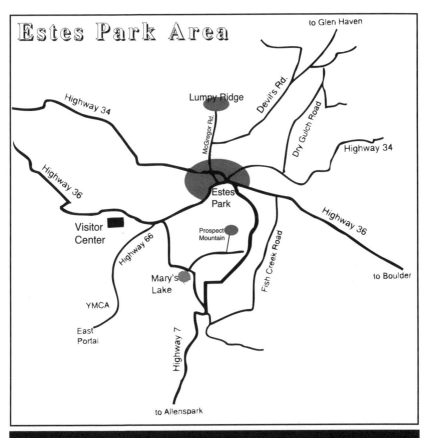

Estes Park Area

- to Glen Haven
- Highway 34
- Lumpy Ridge
- Devil's Rd.
- McGregor Rd.
- Dry Gulch Road
- Highway 34
- Highway 36
- Estes Park
- Visitor Center
- Highway 66
- Prospect Mountain
- Fish Creek Road
- Highway 36
- to Boulder
- Mary's Lake
- YMCA
- East Portal
- Highway 7
- to Allenspark

INTRODUCTION

Climbing in Rocky Mountain National Park is an amazing but committing experience. Alpine rock climbing becomes more popular each year and the Park certainly feels this increase. Special caution needs to be exercised in the mountains. The following *Alpine Rock 101* offers many tips for climbing in the mountain environment.

Lumpy Ridge, just outside of Estes Park, is the crown jewel of multi-pitch cragging in the Park and offers a less committing primer for the high peaks. The weather is usually more hospitable and the routes are often cleaner, less devious, and shorter than their higher neighbors.

One major difference between the high country and most other crags is the lack of established rappel routes. If you're forced to rappel at Lumpy, you will almost certainly have to leave gear behind. Alpine routes often have more "bail stations" but these are a far cry from the sport crag's double bolt lowering stations. Though efforts have been made to reduce the Diamond, Petit Grepon, and Chiefshead to "crag" status with recent rappel routes, most of the time you'll have to walk, scramble, and find a proper mountain descent. Even the aforementioned rap routes won't be accessible from neighboring routes.

ALPINE ROCK 101
(by Fred Knapp —a similar article by the author appeared in *Climbing Magazine #169*)

Franz and Johann accidentally enrolled in an accelerated program at the School of Hard Knocks. Unaware of the prerequisite requirements they found themselves in a field course of Alpine Rock 101, feeling more like lab rats than students. As the thundering roar of their professor echoed through the high peaks, Johann —climbing near his ability and burdened by a rucksack— inched his way up the suddenly soaking granite.

Having no way to haul a pack, Franz was stuck at the belay without rain gear, and only now —when he was thoroughly soaked— had it arrived. As the pair prepared for retreat, an epiphany struck Johann: two Gri-Gri's, a single rope, and six long pitches beneath them would make the descent more painful and tedious than a Barry Manilow double album. Franz tried tapping the rands of his Mythos three times but it didn't take him back to Kansas.

Despite some initial setbacks, such as a routefinding error on the second pitch and a prolonged struggle with a stuck nut on pitch four, the pair decided to continue to the summit. Had the thunderstorm come a few hours earlier, Franz and Johann might have been drinking beer at the Notchtop Cafe. As it now stood, they faced the prospect of a dozen single rope rappels, half of which required setting their own anchors. They should have read the syllabus: Bring two ropes and warm clothes. Arrive on time or be punished.

Unfortunately the School of Hard Knocks is currently the only institute of higher learning offering a Bachelor of Alpinism. Though I recommend some tutoring and a host of fine textbooks, I'll leave you with some Cliff Notes:

BEFORE YOU GO:

•HIT THE BOOKS: Cross reference as many guidebooks as you can. A guidebook that employs a topo format might differ from one that uses photo overlays or detailed written descriptions. Authors might also offer various insights on pitches, or in some cases might differ on grades. (Of course, this guidebook is probably the one you should buy).

•DO YOUR HOMEWORK: Ask mountain shop employees, friends, etc. for information. Focus your questions around trouble spots: Is it easy to get off route? If so, where? Are there distinguishing features to aim for? Does fixed gear sucker you off route? Tips for the descent? Where can we find water on the approach, the descent?

•THE BEST LAID PLANS... Plan ahead with your partner. Under what circumstances will you bail? By what time do you want to be at the halfway point? How do you split the cost of gear left behind? Better to figure this out at the onset and have a cohesive game plan in the event of an emergency. Even a time consuming bout with a stuck nut might be worth $3.00 each. ($12.00/hour?).

•DO YOU SEE WHAT I SEE? Carry small binoculars to the base, especially if you're bivying. Often you can scope the route from the ground so you won't be confused on the wall.

BE PREPARED:

•LONGER IS BETTER: Carry a large supply of over-the-shoulder length runners. The wandering nature of alpine routes eats up long slings which are often needed for belays. Triple them up and they can replace your sport draws. A cordolet also comes in handy.

•TIE THE KNOT: Don't be scared of tying the knot. While you might prefer the sleeker design of the sewn runners, their shortcomings are obvious when you're forced to retreat. In addition to being more expensive, sport draws can't easily be threaded through old pitons or tunnel threads, nor can they be used to back up tattered slings on an established anchor.

•PUT ON A HEX: They're lighter than friends, work better in certain instances, and are easier to part with if the need arises. In fact, take along several of your least favorite pieces so that you'll be more inclined to beef up retreat anchors in a pinch.

•HANDLING YOUR TOOL: Make a hand-held ice axe out of your nut tool by attaching it to a biner with radiator hose clamps. This weighs the same on your harness as a regular nut tool/biner combo, but gives you an ice axe, a heavier swing weight for stuck pieces, and the ability to use the biner as a hammer on cemented gear.

•TWO ROPES GET YOU OFF: Even if you're not into bondage. Two ropes are a blessing if you're forced to retreat, and are often necessary for the descent. A number of two rope systems can be employed. Traditional double rope technique allows you to carry two lighter cords (or one long 300'+ cord). They let you alternate clips, keeping down rope drag on meandering pitches. The drawback, though, is that you can't haul gear unless you pull the rope through your pieces, which puts marginal placements in danger of taking a plunge. I prefer a 10mm lead rope coupled with an 8 or 9mm trail rope. A light trail rope allows the leader to pull up gear that may have been left at the belay, or haul up warm clothing or his partner's pack. For hauling purposes, I don't like a 7mm as it's hard on the hands. No matter what system you choose, don't have the second haul a rope; if it gets stuck, the knock will be very hard.

•WATER WATER EVERYWHERE, BUT NOT A DROP TO DRINK... Carry a water purification system or iodine tablets. Often you can find water on the route. Use wide mouth bottles with an attached lid. Wide-mouths let you add snow to your water, and the attached lid ensures you won't drop the cap.

•THE ESSENTIALS: Headlamps with fresh batteries (tape the switch so it won't accidentally flip on), extra clothes, rainwear, light gloves (polypro liners), helmet, hat (a balaclava is lighter, warmer, fits under a helmet, or can be rolled into a hat), and sunscreen. Sounds like a lot, but all this (excepting the helmet) could fit in the lid of a small pack.

TRICKS OF THE TRADE

•MAKING BAIL: While it may be tempting to feed a rappel directly through webbing, it's better to leave behind an old biner to ensure the ropes won't get pinched or stuck if the webbing twists. Also consider using a modern sticht plate —such as the ATC or Jaws— as these keep lines from twisting and allow climbers to move the knot more easily.

•TO PEE OR NOT TO PEE: Overhydrate. Better to pee at every belay than get altitude sickness. Chewing antacid tablets can also help altitude newcomers cope with the high acidity levels brought on by higher elevations.

•THE CHEAT SHEET: Laminate your topo with clear contact paper and hang it from your harness with a small piece of cord so it is accessible at all times. Mark the topo with the pertinent information gained from your inquiries.

•TAKE TURNS: Don't swing leads, rather take leads in clumps: "You lead the first four pitches; I'll lead the next four." Swinging leads is highly inefficient, especially at altitude because it forces each climber to climb two pitches in a row without physical or mental rest. It's much better to get into a groove of leading or following.

And what of Franz and Johann? They lucked out when an experienced team took pity on them, taught them the Muenter-hitch rappel, and let them rap on their double ropes. And back at the bar that night, Franz and Johann discovered yet another pitfall of their lack of alpine savvy—the rounds were on them.

FOOD, GEAR, CAMPING

If you find yourself —like Franz and Johann— owing meals and beer, check out one of these fine establishments (keeping in mind that advertisers helped bring you this book for less than ten bucks): Notchtop Cafe (healthy food, microbrews, and climber ambiance), Estes Park Brewery, Ed's Cantina (Mexican), Mama Rosa's (Italian), The Dunraven Inn (Italian), Rocky Mountain Fruit Shake (smoothies).

Should you need to replace gear, Colorado Wilderness Sports has a great selection and a knowledgable and friendly staff, as do many stores in nearby Boulder: The Boulder Mountaineer, Neptune Mountaineering, Mountain Sports, and EMS. The Mountain Shop in Fort Collins is near the awesome bouldering at Horsetooth. Exceptional Denver area climbing shops include The Mountain Miser and The Bent Gate in Golden.

Private campgrounds near Estes Park include the KOA east of Estes on Highway 34, The Mary's Lake Campground, south of town on Mary's Lake Road, and the Estes Park Campground west of Estes Park on Spur 66.

LUMPY RIDGE

Malcolm Daly on the first ascent of *Between the Sheets*
M.Daly collection

Trad...

and proud of it.

TRANGO
EXTRAORDINARY CLIMBING GEAR

www.trango.com

800.860.3653

LUMPY RIDGE

Lumpy Ridge contains the greatest concentration of climbing in the park. The nature of the granite, the multitude of long crack systems, and the predominant southern exposure make it the most popular destination. The ridge dominates the northern edge of the Estes valley, and is quite obvious from many vantage points around town.

To get to Lumpy Ridge, take the Hwy 34 bypass north from the intersection of Hwy 34 & 36. Follow this for a short distance until you come to an intersection. Turn right following the sign that directs you to MacGregor Ranch. Follow this road (you'll have great views of Twin Owls along the way) until it makes a pronounced bend right. At the bend is a large entrance gate for the MacGregor Ranch. Drive through the gate and follow the road until you cross the park boundary. There is a decent sized parking lot (which fills up fairly early in the summer), and three trails which head out of the lot to the crags.

This section deals with Lumpy Ridge, starting at the eastern end with the Crescent Wall, then heads west, ending up with Sundance Buttress.

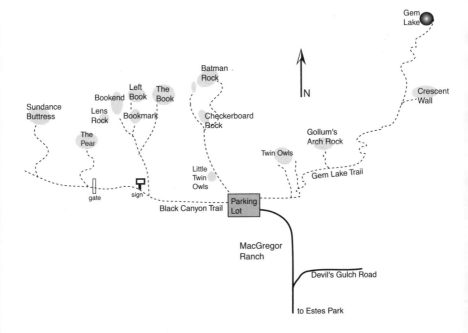

Crescent Wall

The Crescent Wall is only a little over a mile from the parking lot, but its isolated nature provides a unique experience on the sometimes crowded Ridge.

Follow the Gem Lake Trail from the eastern end of the lot for a mile until a sharp left bend in the trail is reached. Head off into a talus and boulder strewn gully which terminates at the base of the wall.

The wall is divided horizontally into two sections, the dividing line being the prominent roof that runs across two thirds of the crag.

Flight for Life (5.12a) begins off the left end of a ledge that sits in the middle of the lower portion of the face. Scramble up broken terrain below and right of the ledge to reach it, then climb past six bolts, angling left at first, then heading right to the roof. Turn the roof (11c), clip a final bolt, then head up to the two bolt anchor. 80 feet in all.

Pressure Drop (5.11a) is a sustained line that begins one hundred or so feet left of the **Crescent Arch** dihedral that curves up the right side of the lower wall.

Climb the finger and hand crack for fifty feet, then head up and right along a traverse. The pitch ends at a rappel stance below two bolts (which can be followed at 5.13 to meet the top of the "Crescent Arch" dihedral. Please note: following these bolts will put you out of single-rope rappel range. The rap from the first stance is 80'.

Crescent Wall

1. Flight For Life 5.12a   2. Pressure Drop 5.11a   3. Finger Lickin' Good 5.11a

Finger Lickin' Good (5.11a) starts up a thin crack 30 feet right of **Pressure Drop**, then heads right using another thin crack and various face holds. Belay where the crack stops traversing and heads straight up. The next pitch follows this finger crack (crux) up to the **Pressure Drop** belay. Rappel 80 feet to the ground.

Gollum's Arch Rock

Gollum's Arch is the prominent rock just east and about the same elevation as the base of Twin Owls. It can be identified by a signature arching dihedral in the middle of the lower face.

Approach via the Gem Lake Trail, passing below Twin Owls. Head left off the trail keeping an eye out for a sign upon encountering a forested ravine.

Descend from all routes by heading west to a 4th class gully.

Gollum's Arch (5.10a) is the classic route on this nice compact crag. Begin with easy friction (just left of the big tree at mid-face) up to a fist crack directly below the obvious arch. Ascend a flake/pillar on the left side and cruise the beautiful arch, which begins as a wide crack (#4 Friend or #3 Camalot) and narrows all the way to fingers/thin hands.

Crank the roof (hard 5.9), step left onto easier ground, and head up to a nice belay tree.

Facial Hair (11a) is another outstanding route on this crag. Begin right of Gollum's, hump a flake and then sling it for protection. Follow a 5.10c short crack to a mantle move, then chase three bolts up the face. Finish in a 5.7 corner.

Close Encounters (5.11a) is basically a solid 5.8 route with a gnarly 5.11 roof comprised of rounded, almost frictionless holds. This climb is included in the guide mostly to round out the offerings on this crag.

Begin up one of two 5.8 corners (right of the big tree) that both lead up to the roof/alcove and subsequent dihedral above. Turn the roof via a strenuous lieback, then continue up the corner above which heads right. Belay at its top.

Step left to easy ground and traverse over to the belay tree on **Gollum's Arch**.

Gollum's Arch

1. Gollum's Arch 5.10a   2. Close Encounters 5.11a

TWIN OWLS

Twin Owls is probably the best known Lumpy Ridge landmark, and in my opinion is the most aptly named rock I have ever seen. The Owls cannot be missed from the parking lot, and are accessed via a brief stint on the Gem Lake Trail. Several of the routes are aid lines, and much of the free climbing is on the harder end of the spectrum. A sub-crag to the Owls, known as the Lower Owls, holds some great moderate lines, all of which end on a tilted slab known as the Roosting Ramp. Most of the routes on the Owls proper begin on this ramp, which has a separate access trail.

To approach the Lower Owls, head out of the lot on the Gem Lake Trail, pass through an aspen grove, then break left and pick up a steep trail which winds up to meet the Lower Owls.

Organ Pipes (5.6) is reached by heading left at the bottom of the face until a gully is reached that heads up to the western face. Ascend this gully, then head right at its top and begin from a large ledge. The route ascends the left wall of the massive dihedral all the way to the Roosting Ramp.

The first pitch begins right of the tree and follows a groove for 75 - 80 feet. Continue up and belay from a good stance on the obvious horizontal fissure which bisects the wall.

The second pitch stays close to the corner to keep the rating at 5.6, and heads left at the top to reach another nice belay ledge.

The final pitch ascends the nearby right facing dihedral to the Roosting Ramp.

Descend the Ramp and pick up the trail back to the base.

SOUTH FACE ROUTES:

Approach via the Gem Lake Trail, continuing until a switchback around a large boulder is reached. Head north just before another boulder. Pick up the trail, which heads past a cliff band then ends at the base of the Roosting Ramp.

Crack of Fear (5.10) is one of Lumpy's most infamous routes. This offwidth is feared by many and climbed by few, but it remains a mega classic and historic line. This guide preserves the historically inaccurate sandbag grade.

The route begins at the low end of the Roosting Ramp near a feature called the Rat's Tooth, a detached pillar right at the base of the crack. Above the Rat's Tooth, the crack begins with fists, widens to offwidth, arches left, then fires straight up. An awesome line. Jam up on the left side of the Rat's Tooth, continue up the 5.9 offwidth (if there is such a thing!), pass a pin, then head left to a belay stance (2 bolts) on a flake. It's only a 75 foot rappel from here if you're having second thoughts.

The second pitch attacks the 11a offwidth above. Grunt past 2 more pins then head left via hard 5.10 underclings, regaining the crack where it straightens out again. Belay ten feet up past the undercling moves at a stance.

The third pitch ascends more offwidth (5.10a) for a long pitch, getting easier (5.9) halfway. At the top a ramp leads right and up. Belay at it's upper end. Thankfully, much easier ground finishes left to the summit.

To descend, scramble west to the saddle between the two owls. Head north via a wet, slimy passage. Either down climb a 5.0 route (**Bowels of the Owls**), or rappel 75 feet from slings which are threaded through the pinched off section at the bottom of the passage. Head west until an obvious descent gully is reached.

Wolf's Tooth (5.8) is one of Lumpy's oldest routes, and is certainly one of the top three in its grade. The route ascends the north side of a completely detached pillar that stands at the top of the Roosting Ramp, just off the left shoulder of the West Owl.

Begin up a wide crack (5.8) and follow it until a chimney can be reached. Ascend the chimney (strenuous), clipping various old pitons for pro, then find a belay stance just below the top of the pillar.

Twin Owls- South Face

route climbs behind pillar

Wolf's Tooth

Crack of Fear

A 5.7 pitch up a groove heads left from the belay or a 5.9 pitch up a right facing corner heads right. Both climb to another belay near the top of the West Owl. Easy ground finishes the route.

Descend as for **Crack of Fear**.

The **Pin Route** with the **Sky Route finish** (5.3) is an exceptional climb that scales the northwest shoulder of the West Owl. Approach the climb using the Lower Owls trail (see **Organ Pipes** approach), but stay left, contouring around an outcropping, and climb up to the base of the north face.

The route begins in a chimney on the far right side of the face. Climb up to a ramp on the northwest face, and cross the ramp to a belay stance marked by pins.

The second pitch hand traverses right from the pitons, and belays after a very short distance behind a flake.

The final pitch follows the flakes to the summit (5.3).

East Ridge (5.8) is a very good route that follows the right skyline as viewed from the parking lot. Approach by walking along the Gem Lake Trail past the approaches to other routes. About 500 feet past a massive boulder, the trail curves. At the inside curve follow a path to the base of the route.

Look for a large flake leaning against the East Ridge of the Twin Owls. Climb the flake and at a fixed pin move onto the ridge proper. Continue up cracks to a comfortable ledge and belay.

Pitch 2 climbs around the right-hand side of an A-shaped roof and up a flake and face above.

Descend the Bowels of the Owls.

Little Twin Owls

This fun crag is located due west of the parking lot, and is named for its rough resemblance to the big owls. From the lot, take the upper of two trails (follow the one marked "Climbers Trail" to Batman and Checkerboard Rocks).

"Strappo" Hughes on Little Twin Owl Finger Crack. Photo: Steve "Crusher" Bartlett.

Little Twin Owls Finger Crack
Little Twin Owls Finger Crack (5.11a) is the overhanging finger crack on the south side of the southernmost Little Owl. Hard liebacking on rounded rock gains the difficult crack.

Face Climb (5.11c) A toprope problem that roughly follows the arete right of the Finger Crack.

Both routes can be toproped from chains on the summit. Access to these chains is via a 5.0 climb up the west side of the northern Little Owl.

BATMAN ROCK AREA

Batman Rock

Batman
Pinnacle

Little Twin Owls

Batman Rock

Batman Rock is very conspicuous from the parking lot as it crowns the ridge west of Twin Owls. It's dome-like appearance is unique among the ridge's crags, and on it lie several excellent lines.

To get to Batman, follow the upper trail out of the west end of the lot. The trail splits again at a sign: the left fork goes to Checkerboard Rock, then heads up to Batman Pinnacle and the south face of Batman. The right fork heads up steeper terrain (but on a nice new trail) to the east face climbs. The two trails are specified in the individual route approaches that follow. Descend for all routes by heading north off the summit, then east, picking up a descent gully.

Bat Crack (5.9) is an old classic. The route begins midway up the east face, left of a dead end crack with a tree growing out of it. The crack with the tree is the start of **Spaziergang**. Do not climb into this crack! **Bat Crack** follows the left hand crack, which does not quite reach the ground. Choose a line up into the crack (5.8 face directly underneath, easier to the left), then follow the crack to its end. Head up and left where it dies out (fairly unprotected 5.8), find another short crack, follow it to its termination, then cruise up easier (5.6) but runout face climbing to a belay in slings underneath an obvious notch in the roof band above.

The second pitch liebacks the double roof (solid 5.9), then picks up a finger crack at the lip and follows it to the top.

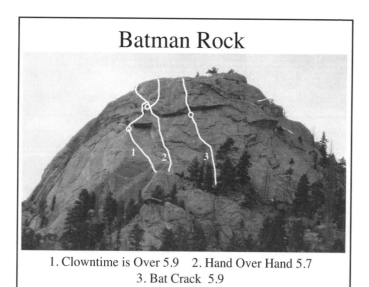

Batman Rock

1. Clowntime is Over 5.9   2. Hand Over Hand 5.7
3. Bat Crack 5.9

100 feet left (downhill) of **Bat Crack** lies the start of **Hand Over Hand** (5.7). The route starts behind a large outcropping, set off from Batman Rock proper, which creates a 3rd class chimney system (allowing access to either face), near a large, distinct triangular face. Begin up a steep but well featured (5.5 or so) face, aiming for a handcrack behind a flake directly above. Ascend the crack (5.6) and belay where it ends below the roof.

Traverse left under the roof for 35 feet, find a weakness in the roof, and climb through (5.7). 30 feet higher is a nice belay ledge with a tree.

The last pitch heads left over 5.6 terrain to the top.

Clowntime Is Over (5.9) is perhaps Batman's most traveled route. Begin on top of the offset outcropping mentioned in **Hand Over Hand**. Lean across the chimney and pull onto the face at a flake (scary, scary, scary 5.7). Continue up and left, aiming for a nice belay flake that sits at the junction of the east and south faces.

The second pitch heads straight up the prow to the looming roof above. Turn the roof (very exciting 5.9) using a large hold to left of the roof's apex. Another 5.9 move is encountered a bit higher at small roof/bulge. Belay on the same ledge mentioned in **Hand Over Hand**.

The last pitch is the same as **Hand Over Hand**, though it is possible to continue up and right through overlaps (5.8)

Batman Pinnacle

Batman Pinnacle is unique amongst Lumpy Ridge formations. It is actually a detached buttress with a pinnacle-like summit pillar. Access to Batman Pinnacle is gained by following the Batman Rock trail out of the lot, then taking the branch that leads to Checkerboard Rock. The trail contours directly below Checkerboard, then turns north and heads into a scree slope. Scramble up the talus and you'll be at the base of Batman Pinnacle.

Batman and Robin (5.6) is a moderate mega-classic that can be enjoyed by climbers of all abilities. The route ascends the entire south face of the pinnacle, which is actually very tall (350 feet). Look for two dead trees near the base. This is where the route begins. Climb up into a broken left facing corner system using any one of many starts. The easiest climbs up and right (5.5), but a more aesthetic start ascends a face to a shallow left facing corner to the left of the easier start. Belay atop a flake at a cramped but good stance approximately 65 feet up.

The next pitch traverses right (sparse pro) to a bigger right facing dihedral which is followed (5.4) up to its broken top. A variation climbs straight up off the first belay (5.8, no pro), then picks up a crack which leads back right to the top of the broken corner. Either way, belay atop the corner where it ends.

The third pitch tackles the middle of three cracks (5.6) leading straight off the belay stance. The crack is flared and somewhat difficult to protect, but certainly not impossible. The crack to the right is a nice 5.7 variation. Both end up in an alcove below a little roof. Turn the roof on the left, then cruise up easier terrain to a belay below the western face of the summit block.

The final pitch ascends the face to the top.

To descend, rappel to the north from slings through a tunnel. Scramble down to the west, follow the gully south, and rappel again to the south from slings around a boulder. This is a 80 foot rappel, and heads down the western side of Bat Flake, a detached buttress just west of Batman Pinnacle.

Rap one final time from slings around a horn to the ground (80 feet). This rap is about half way up Bat Flake's south face.

Bat Flake

Bat Flake is the obvious huge flake just left of Batman Pinnacle. It is approached the same as the Pinnacle.

The route **Bat Flake** (5.10b or .11a) starts up any of the easy (5.5 or 5.6) shallow corner and flake systems that populate the rock below the flake proper. Belay on sloping terrain before the route steepens.

The next pitch heads right up a shallow left facing corner, then heads left over a small roof to a bolt. Head left and up again to another bolt (heading right to a different bolt provides a 5.10b variation). Continue straight up (crux), passing another bolt and a pin in a crack. A final bolt is passed before reaching a crack (#3.5 Friend protects this nicely) which heads to the summit.

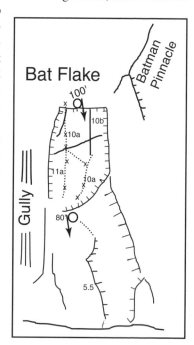

Descend by rappeling 100 feet to the first belay stance from anchors on top of the flake. A second rappel of half a rope length puts you on the ground.

Checkerboard Rock

Checkerboard Rock is a good-sized outcropping which is encountered on the trail to Batman Pinnacle before the Pinnacle itself is reached. It sits to the south of the entire Batman Rock formation.

A chimney cuts directly up the middle of the face, and a ledge (Surrey Ledge) breaks horizontally across the entire width of the rock. These two features create the "checkerboard" appearance of the buttress.

Ziggie's Day Out (5.10d) begins on the far left side of Checkerboard's south face near a large boulder. Head right via underclings using a flake. Pick up a thin crack at the end and follow it as it zig-zags (but keep bearing right) until a small roof band ends, and the crack shoots straight up (crux). The difficulties continue all the way to Surrey Ledge. Belay on the ledge.

Move left a little until a right-leaning crack is reached. Ascend the crack, then head straight up where it intersects a vertical crack. 5.9 terrain leads to the summit.

Descend by walking off the summit to the west.

Crystal Catch (5.9) is another great Checkerboard route at an easier grade.

Start near a small flake below a shallow right facing dihedral at the low point of the south face. Climb into the corner and attack the crux bulge. Head right on crystals to a left-facing corner/flake. Follow it up to a belay between two small flake spikes.

The next pitch heads straight up 5.7 grooves and face to Surrey Ledge. From here, take the middle of three obvious grooves (5.7) to a right facing flake/corner. Either head right up the flake or left up another groove to the summit.

1. Crystal Catch   2. Ziggie's Day Out

The Book

Without a doubt, the Book is Lumpy's most visited crag, and deservedly so. There are so many high quality routes that fit the "classic" description that narrowing it down to the top lines is truly a stiff challenge.

Approach by following the Black Canyon Trail west out of the lot, then turn right onto the approach trail at a sign announcing "The Book".

The Book is split into easily identifiable sections. A giant dihedral cuts up the middle of the Book. This landmark is called the Howling At The Wind dihedral, in reference to the route which ascends the corner. To the right of the dihedral is a stunning slab, graced by several excellent cracks, the most famous of which is **J Crack**. To the left is the aptly named Pages Wall.

The routes from **J Crack** to **Femp** exit with a shared pitch referred to as the **Cave Exit**. The Cave, which is actually a left facing corner and alcove sits above J Crack and is visible from the ground. It is the easiest and most direct exit from the right side Book routes. We have also included information and topos on the more difficult exit routes: **Final Chapter, Cheap Date**, and **Outlander**. These provide excellent, more direct but longer finishes in the 5.10 range.

To return to the base from the left-hand routes, head east down some big slabs off the summit, then head south through a deadfall area. Some easy scrambling puts one on top of the **Cave Exit** area. From the **Cave Exit**, downclimb a steep gully just east of the **Cave Exit**. Follow ramps and grooves to the east and south. There is no need to rappel if you follow the worn path.

THE BOOK GROUP

The Book

Left Book

Bookmark

Pages Wall

J Crack slab

J Crack Slab Routes

Femp (5.9) is one of the many stellar crack climbs found on the right side of the Book. The approach trail ends at the base of the Book and just left of the start to **Femp**.

Begin up moderate terrain (5.5) just left of an obvious gully then head up and left to a ledge which lies just below the crack itself. Belay.

Head off the right end of the ledge into the crack, following past a pin (5.9) onto easier terrain (5.7), then back into a short 5.9 facing corner. Belay at the top of the corner. Note: this is a very long pitch.

The next pitch heads left over a left facing corner until a left leaning crack is reached. This is actually the fourth pitch of a climb called **Endless Crack**, but it keeps the rating consistent and is the most frequently used final pitch. Head up the crack to a slot/break in the roof band that runs across the right side of the Book. Turn the roof using a wedged flake (5.9+), then head left to the top of the Cave.

An easier (5.7) but less aesthetic line (also the original finish) heads up and left from the belay to a thin crack below an arch. Climb up into the arch, then break right, aiming for a weakness in the roof band on the left side. Follow the path of least resistance and join the previous finish on top of the Cave. This finish is called Right Exit.

J Crack (5.9 or .11c) is one of Lumpy's most heavily traveled and enjoyable routes. It is one of the quintessential crack climbs on the ridge, and shouldn't be missed if ability and time permits.

The route begins left of a feature called the Cavity (which lies left of the Femp gully) and ascends 5.6 terrain into a groove which is followed up past a slot (5.7) and up onto the left end of Femp's ledge. Belay.

Traverse left (exciting and thin 5.8) into the bottom of the J, and cruise the flawless crack past a pin (5.9) to a belay in a pod/alcove.

The next pitch requires a choice. Either continue up the crack through the headwall above (5.11c on RPs) and belay on the ledge; continue up the crack but traverse right below the headwall (5.10a, absolutely no pro) into an easy corner, then back up and left to the same belay; or traverse left (5.9, also no pro) just above the pod belay to a 5.8 crack (which is the second pitch of a route called **Visual Aids**). The two traverses can be decently protected by placing gear high in the crack before committing to the traverses. This makes it especially exciting for the second, however.

If one of the first two options were chosen, the next pitch heads left off the belay ledge over easy (5.2) ground, then up to the cave. If the **Visual Aids** exit was chosen, climb the 5.8 crack to a cramped belay.

Now traverse right over 5.0 ground to pick up the headwall escapes and climb to the cave.

   Loose Ends (5.9) is another Book classic that encompasses four pitches of varied terrain.

   Begin in a shallow left facing dihedral just left of the start to J Crack, and

climb it via perfect finger jams (solid 5.9). At its top, head left via underclings to a ramp and belay a short ways up the ramp in a nice pocket.

   The next pitch heads left again to the second of two vertical finger cracks (the first one encountered goes at 5.10b) and climb it (5.9) past a right arching corner and up onto a ledge near a flake. Belay.

   The third pitch climbs straight up a nicely featured face into a big left facing (and left leaning) dihedral. 5.9 liebacking leads to a large ledge. Belay.

   The final pitch traverses up and right to reach the Cave.

J CRACK AREA ROUTES

1. Femp
2. J Crack
3. Loose Ends
4. Pear Buttress
5. Thindependence

Pear Buttress (5.8+) begins where the approach trail ends. The route starts up the right side of the huge flake that leans against the wall. Either climb in from the right (5.7 face, no pro) or tackle a crack directly below the right edge of the flake (5.9, but often wet and slimy). After the flake is gained, follow it up to the top, then ascend the twin cracks (5.8+) which lead up from the right end of the flake. Belay in the same pod that **Loose Ends** uses.

Now traverse left along the ramp to the edge of the wall, then head up and right to a nice ledge. Belay.

The third pitch ascends the amazing crack straight above. When the roof is encountered, undercling right and again share a belay on the same ledge **Loose Ends** uses after its third pitch. Once again, easy ground leads to the cave.

Thindependence (5.10c) is a short route, but is worth doing if you're up at the Book anyway and want to get in one more pitch before you head home.

Start on top of the giant flake mentioned in **Pear Buttress**. This is easily gained via scrambling up the left side (third class), but the first pitch of **Pear Buttress** is nicer. Take the twin finger crack which leads off the left side of the ledge (crux), then pick up another crack which heads right and continue up to the first Pear Buttress belay.

Now traverse left to the edge of the buttress, then downclimb or scramble to a rappel station (slings) below. One 60 ft. rappel puts you back on the ground.

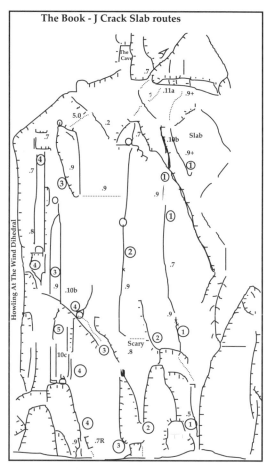

The Book - J Crack Slab routes

Book Exits (from right to left):

Cave Exit (5.8) This is the somewhat tricky, yet easiest, way to leave the wall. The climbing is exciting and exposed but is not sustained. From the cave belay, boulder out the wall and out a small roof passing a fixed pin.

The next three routes are all on the headwall of the Book called the Exit Wall. They provide difficult alternatives to the Cave Exit.

Final Chapter (5.11a) provides an exquisite finish to any route on the Book. It begins below the Cave and off the right side of Fang Ledge, allowing easy access if exiting to the Cave isn't in the plans. One can also traverse right along the ledge (spot of 5.5) to reach the starting point.

Begin below the right facing corner which makes up the left border of the Cave and face climb into a 5.9 crack which leads to a small ledge. From the ledge, take the right hand fissure and follow it up past a pronounced left fork. Note: the crux of the crack occurs at a very thin spot protected by RPs, etc. Where the crack dies out, head a little up and left to pick up another 5.9 crack which leads to a nice belay ledge.

Fourth class terrain out right leads down to terrain above the Cave, or climb 5.6 rock up and right of the belay to the summit.

Joyce Bracht
on Cave Exit
Steve Bartlett photo

Cheap Date (5.10b), an excellent climb, begins in the same place as **Final Chapter**. Climb the crack to the small ledge, but take the left crack. The two cracks diverge, and **Cheap Date** leans left. The crux occurs where a shallow left facing corner begins. Finish on the same ledge as **Final Chapter**, and pick an exit.

Outlander (5.10d) is a 2-pitch finish that begins just left of the previous two routes and heads up the left facing corner (5.9), following it up as it arches left and meets another dihedral, forming an A-shaped roof. Turn the roof at its center and continue up the thin crack above (10b). A final, easier corner leads to the small belay ledge shared with the previous two routes.

Either pick one of the previous two finishes or traverse left to another thin crack (5.10d) which heads up to a left facing corner and the summit.

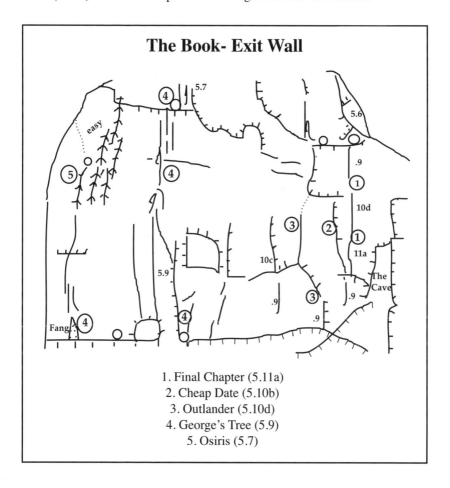

The Book- Exit Wall

1. Final Chapter (5.11a)
2. Cheap Date (5.10b)
3. Outlander (5.10d)
4. George's Tree (5.9)
5. Osiris (5.7)

Left Side of The Book

The following routes are on the left side of the Book. Use the regular approach trail, but head west where it terminates below the J Crack slab.

Howling At The Wind (5.11b) climbs straight up the landmark dihedral and attacks the obvious roof 150 feet off the ground. Bring large (#3-#4) Friends for the first pitch.

Begin at a pillar and follow the right hand split of the crack into the dihedral. Lieback the long corner (strenuous 5.9) to a belay at a wedged flake.

The second pitch follows the remainder of the dihedral to the roof, then undercling out to the left and turn it (5.11b). Continue up 10b terrain to a decent belay between two left facing dihedrals.

Finally, follow either corner (both 5.9) up, then right at their tops over easy ground to the Cave.

El Camino Real (5.12c) is one of the ridge's hardest routes, and is a free climbing gem. The route ascends the right wall of the Howling At The Wind dihedral, following a stunning crack all the way.

Begin with Howling... at the pillar. Climb the crack above, and take the right hand split where it forks. An awkward stem right where the crack again heads straight up puts one at the bottom of El Camino Real. There is a fixed nut at the base of the crack.

Jam the crack past another nut, three bolts (crux), and a nut to a belay at two coldshuts.

A 100 foot rappel reaches the ground.

Corner Pump Station (5.11c) begins 125 feet off the ground. Do the first pitch of Howling... and belay at the wedged flake.

Now traverse right to a pod a little above the coldshuts on Camino Real. Plenty of exposure and excitement. Ascend the dual cracks above past a pin (crux). Take the left crack where the right one terminates, and continue up to a 10b undercling which is followed by an 11a move at its end. Continue up to the twin dihedral belay on Howling....

The last pitch follows either corner to easier ground and the Cave.

Perelandra (5.11a) begins at the very same pillar but takes the left fork of the crack and follows it up (spot of 5.10) to a belay stance just below and left of the wedged flake belay noted on the previous routes.

The second pitch heads straight up to a hanging flake, which can be liebacked on the left. Now head right, turn the roof (crux) and cross the top of Howling's... roof. Continue up to the twin corner belay.

Ascend either corner and head to the Cave.

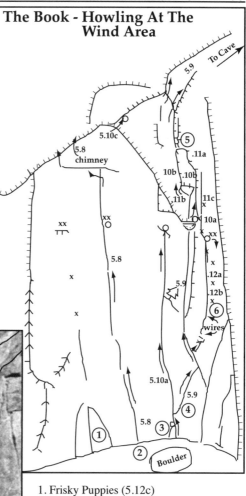

The Book - Howling At The Wind Area

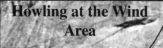

1. Frisky Puppies (5.12c)
2. Fat City (5.10c)
3. Perelandra (5.11a)
4. Howling at the Wind (5.11b)
5. Corner Pump Station (5.11c)
6. El Camino Real (5.12c)

Fat City (5.10c) always ranks at or near the top of any Lumpy Ridge climber's list of favorites. The route heads straight up to the huge arch roof in the middle of the face, left of Howling. Begin up the crack directly below the roof and follow it (5.8) to a piton and bolt anchor. Belay.

Continue up the crack as it narrows (5.10a at the top), then traverse left along the crack. Head up and right via a tight slot, then turn the roof at its apex (crux). Belay just above.

The third pitch follows a long series of flakes (continuous 5.9) up and right to the Cave. A great link-up combines this route with Outlander and Cheap Date for a very sustained 5.10 route.

Frisky Puppies (5.12b) is another Lumpy testpiece that lies to the left and downhill of the Howling... area routes.

Locate the first of ten bolts just off the ground, and follow them up beautiful rock passing a horn en route (sling helpful). The crux occurs between the third and fourth bolt. The bolts end under the roof. Turn the roof (small wires or TCUs protect it) and belay at a horn. Rappel 165 feet to the ground.

Pages Wall photo

1. Osiris (5.7)
2. George's Tree (5.9)
3. Fat City (5.10)

The start to **George's Tree** (5.9) could hardly be more obvious. The route begins up the beautiful crack which reaches the ground to the left of Frisky Puppies. Follow the crack (5.9), which varies from fists to hands and passes a tree, all the way to an obvious belay ledge a little under a rope length off the ground. The crack is a great introduction to Lumpy Ridge's flared cracks —protection is a bit tricky and jams require a bit more thought.

The second pitch heads up off the left side of the ledge over a broken corner (5.5) for 50 feet. Break right into a right leaning crack and follow it to a belay where another distinct crack heads straight up.

The third pitch ascends the 5.8 crack (spot of 5.9 near the top) all the way to the big ledge (Fang Ledge). Belay near a small tree.

Next, climb the right hand crack which leads out of an alcove area near the belay tree. Where the crack peters out, keep switching cracks (always moving right) and climb to a ledge just below the summit.

The final pitch climbs the 5.7 corner that leads off the right side of the ledge to the summit.

Osiris (5.7) is rated as a moderate, but be ready for some pretty stiff 5.7 climbing. The route is an indisputable classic, however, and shouldn't be missed.

Begin in the chimney to the left of **George's Tree** and ascend it to the top (5.6). Belay on the ledge.

The second pitch climbs the broken 5.5 corner up and left to a belay on a ledge with a tree. The higher up the belay is set, the better the chance of reaching Fang Ledge on the next long lead.

Either climb the corner or the crack on the right (both 5.6-5.7 range), and pick up twin cracks near the top. Follow one of these (both hard 5.7) to Fang Ledge.

Move left along the ledge to "The Fang," a pointed pillar on the ledge. Climb the Fang and head up the leftmost crack off the top of the pillar. Follow it up through a bulge (more hard 5.7) and cruise it to a tree. Belay.

A fifth pitch (5.2) heads up the left side of the wall to the summit.

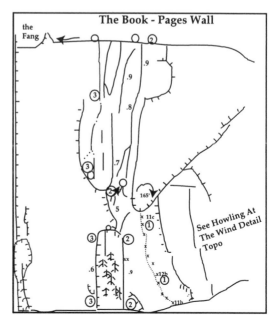

The Book - Pages Wall

Approach **Living Dead** (5.11b) by first locating a 6 inch offwidth on the right wall as you enter the cleft. Two cracks to its left is the **Living Dead** crack. Ascend the crack as it heads left, then attack the difficult crux section of the crack via liebacking. Belay at a horn with slings. A 70 foot rappel reaches the ground from here if one has had enough.

The next pitch continues up the crack (5.9) to a left facing corner. Follow this (10a/b) to another good belay horn.

A double rope rappel puts you back on the ground.

Dead Boy Direct (5.11d) begins up the dihedral left of **Living Dead**. Climb the 5.9 corner, then strike out left and up into a thin crack two-thirds of the way up. The difficult crack continues up, then heads right to join **Living Dead** near the bottom of the 10a dihedral on the second pitch. Belay at the horn with slings.

Double rope rappel to descend.

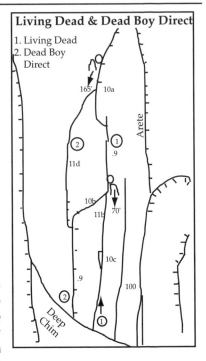

Living Dead & Dead Boy Direct

1. Living Dead
2. Dead Boy Direct

Renaissance Wall (5.12b) is one of the newer bolted lines on the ridge. This route lies in the next deep cleft west of the previously mentioned one. Contour west below the buttress that separates them (the Isis Buttress), then head up into the chasm.

On the right hand wall as you enter the cleft, locate a bolt below a left arching crack. Climb up to the first bolt, then make a decision. Either continue up to another bolt and into the crack (5.11a), or head up and left past six more bolts (10a). Both variations end at the same two bolt anchor.

The next pitch climbs up past fifteen more bolts (steep 12b) to another two bolt anchor just below the Isis Buttress ridge line.

Rap 140 feet to the first anchor, then another 70 feet or so to the ground.

Renaissance Wall

.12b

10a   11a

10c

The Bookmark

The Bookmark sits just south of the Book, and derives its name from its position between the Book and the Left Book (thereby creating a bookmark). The Bookmark is not as popular as the Book, but the rock is just as good and the routes are of the same caliber. There is a large detached crag to the east of the Bookmark which forms a nice climbing area in its own right. This is the Bookmark Pinnacle, and is detailed after the section on the Bookmark. The two crags are separated by a gully, making each rock distinctive.

Approach the Bookmark the same as the Book, but follow signs where a separate trail splits left off the Book trail.

To descend from all summit routes, rappel north (towards the Left Book) from a tree near the summit. This rap ends in a gully between the Bookmark and the Left Book. From here, either rappel or scramble (4th class) to the west down the gully and pick up the Left Book trail that contours around the west side of the Bookmark.

Backflip (5.9) is on the south face of the Bookmark. Begin the route 25 feet left of the gully separating the Bookmark from the Bookmark Pinnacle. Ascend a nice right facing flake to a 5.8+ corner. After the corner ends, there is a nice flat ledge. Belay here.

The next pitch is short, and heads up 5.6 rock straight off the left end of the ledge. Belay below an obvious right arching corner on the big ledge (Library Ledge) which traverses two thirds of the south face.

The third pitch climbs the corner above, then cuts right at a nice flake (hard 5.8) just below the roof/arch. Keep traversing right and belay at a good stance among broken rock.

The next pitch heads right off the belay and climbs into a 5.9 crack. Pass a piton and follow the steepening crack until it ends. Where it does, head right to a groove, which can be followed up to a belay on the ridge line.

Descend to the east, then south down the Bookmark Pinnacle gully, utilizing a large tree for an anchor. Scramble down the remainder of the gully to the base.

Romulan Territory (5.10a) is the finest route on the Bookmark, and should not be missed if ability permits. The route begins from Library Ledge, so we recommend utilizing **Backflip** as an approach.

Once on the ledge, traverse left to a shallow corner just left of **Backflip's** arching dihedral. Ascend this corner past a bulge (10a). At the top of the corner, step left and belay below the massive dihedral that runs up the middle of the upper face.

The next pitch ascends the dihedral itself (5.9). Where it arches to the right there are two options. Continue right via underclings to the ridge line (5.9) and belay or turn the roof and head straight up to the summit.

Melvin's Wheel (5.8+) is another fantastic tour of the Bookmark. The route actually begins around the western side of the crag and winds around to the south side and up to the summit. Follow the trail below the south face, and hike uphill towards the Left Book. Look to the right and enter a big alcove created by the intersection of a leaning buttress on the lower south face and the west buttress itself. Begin up the left facing corner marked by a large tree at its base. Ascend this feature and head right toward the obvious roof. Turn the roof via the crack (5.8), then

The Bookmark

5.10a finish

1

2

1. Romulan Territory
2. Backflip

keep moving up and right to a belay on Library Ledge (on the south face).

The next pitch climbs the only crack in the middle of the beautiful slab (5.7 at the bottom, 5.8+ near the top). Set up a belay below the chimney (the crack terminates here).

Turn the bulge above (5.8+), enter the chimney, and head to the summit.

Fantasy Ridge (5.9) never seems to have much traffic, but I don't understand why. It is one of the ridge's classic 5.9s, and every pitch offers varied and flawless rock.

Begin uphill from **Melvin's Wheel** at a left leaning hand crack which is reached by face climbing in from the left. Cruise the crack for 40 feet or so until a move around to the south face can be made. Belay below at the base of a short crack which is directly below a single bolt.

The next pitch climbs the crack then continues up to the bolt. After clipping it, head up a few more feet (5.9), then break right to a 5.5 right facing corner. Climb this feature and belay at its top.

The next pitch heads up and right into an alcove. Now head straight up to the roof. Either turn the roof on the right or left (5.9 and 5.8, respectively). Above is a very thin crack, which is climbed until a traverse out right below the roof can be made. The higher you go in the crack before traversing, the harder the traverse. Belay below another nice crack.

Ascend the crack above (5.9). The difficulties end upon reaching the top of the block split by the crack. 5.2 climbing from here reaches the summit.

Between The Sheets (5.11c) is an old aid line that utilizes the first two pitches of **Fantasy...** as an approach. From the second belay head up to the ledge with boulders via a groove. Find a flake below a left facing corner on the upper west face. Climb into the corner, and where it arches left, mantle up into a finger crack. Follow this up (5.10b) until a horizontal fissure is encountered. Traverse slightly right here, then up again into a much smaller crack. Climb this difficult feature (5.11c, at least) to a belay at two old bolts. Please back up the bolts.

Next, traverse right into another horizontal crack and continue until a 5.10d move can be made onto the arête. Climb straight up past two more bolts to the top of the block and then on to the summit.

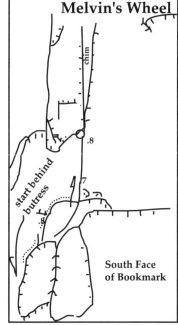

Melvin's Wheel

South Face
of Bookmark

Bookmark Pinnacle

The Bookmark Pinnacle is the detached buttress just southeast of the Bookmark. It is readily identifiable by the unique spire/pinnacle formation which juts straight up from its upper reaches.

Both of the routes included here ascend the pinnacle on their final pitch, which is an objective well worth obtaining. The top of the pinnacle is akin to the summit of a desert spire, and provides a unique perspective as well as a rare treat for Lumpy Ridge.

Approach the Bookmark Pinnacle by following the signs to the Bookmark, then head east along the base of the Bookmark until the Pinnacle is reached.

Descend from the summit by making a free rappel to the north. Once on the ground, rappel again to the east down the obvious chimneys. You may opt to downclimb these (5.5 or so), but I've always found rappelling much faster. An easy scramble at the bottom of the chimneys puts you back at the base.

Cave Route (5.7) is the easiest route to the summit, and many a climber has returned to tell great tales of the exciting exposure while climbing the pinnacle's arête.

Begin by climbing the descent chimneys detailed in the descent information. These begin way up the east side of the formation. Near the top of the chimney on the north wall find a 5.7 handcrack which is followed to the Upper Terrace (the large ledge directly below the pinnacle itself). Belay.

The next pitch ascends the south edge of the pinnacle (5.7 and plenty of exposure!) to the summit.

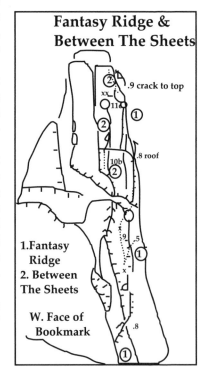

**Fantasy Ridge &
Between The Sheets**

.9 crack to top

.8 roof

1.Fantasy
   Ridge
2. Between
   The Sheets

W. Face of
   Bookmark

East Side (5.8+) is another summit route which begins downhill from the descent chimneys (SE corner of the crag) at a nice right-facing dihedral. Climb this (5.7) all the way to the Lower Terrace (the ledge which cuts across the south face). Belay.

The second pitch climbs the rightmost crack through the roof (crux) and follows it left then straight up again to the Upper Terrace. Now climb the south edge of the pinnacle to the top.

Bookmark Pinnacle

Cave Route belay

1. East Side 5.8+
note: Cave Route climbs around the back side of the Bookmark Pinnacle

Left Book

The Left Book is a remarkable slab that lies behind the Bookmark and to the west of the Book. On it are several routes of superior quality, and for the moderate leader or follower it is a haven of easier and well protected climbs. Although the approach is a little longer and steeper than most of the other formations on the ridge, the Lumpy experience is not complete without a trip up to this great cliff.

Approach the Left Book by following the Black Canyon Trail and turning off at the Book sign. Follow the signs to the Bookmark, but walk beneath the south face of the Bookmark and head uphill, passing the western face of the Bookmark. After a short distance, the broad slab of the Left Book will come into view. All of the routes in this guide start near the low point of the rock, or just uphill on the left edge.

Descend by walking west off the large ledge (Paperback Ledge) which cuts across the entire wall at the point where the rock steepens. From here, pick up the obvious gully which heads south and back to the base.

For the first two routes, I recommend using a 60 meter rope, as the second pitches on each are very long, and good belay stances can't be reached with the standard 50 meters.

Hiatus (5.7+) begins at the low point of the crag. Look for a distinctive right facing corner (the others nearby are all left facing) and climb it past a sharp jog right, then up into a thin crack (5.7+). At the end of the crack, traverse up and left towards the left end of the small roof above. Climb past the left end of the roof and up to a nice belay ledge with a tree. This pitch is much longer than it looks from the ground.

The next pitch—another long one— crosses the ledge to its right end and picks up the left side of a conspicuous raised pillar. Climb this long corner (the face of the pillar goes at 5.6, but there is no pro) until it stops. When it does, step left to another arching corner, and follow it to a belay in an alcove beneath a small roof.

The third pitch is a rather nebulous affair. Just head up out of the awkward alcove and head to Paperback Ledge. This pitch is nice and short, which is convenient because I always seem get caught in a thunderstorm at the second belay.

White Whale (5.7) is perhaps the most climbed route on Left Book, which means it still sees less traffic than the Book's trade routes.

Begin in the left facing corner just left of **Hiatus'** start and follow it all the way up to the left edge of the roof, then past it to ledge with the nice belay tree.

The second pitch heads left off the ledge and into a wonderful crack that virtually sucks pro off your rack. Follow this up to a horizontal crack, then head right briefly and pick up the crack as it resumes its trip upward across the slab. This is not particularly difficult climbing (5.6-5.7) but can be deceiving because of the delicate friction required to make progress. Where the crack ends, cross right into the arching dihedral mentioned in "Hiatus" and belay in the same alcove. Warning: this is a 180 ft. pitch.

Pick a finish (none are harder than 5.5 or so) and head to Paperback Ledge. Straight up out of the alcove seems to be the most convenient.

Left Book
1. Hiatus 5.7 2. White Whale 5.7 3. The Dog 5.7
4. Cottontail 5.6 5. Fandango 5.5

The Dog (5.7) is yet another super moderate. Begin up the next flake/corner to the left of **White Whale** and follow it all the way to a small belay ledge between two opposing dihedrals.

The second pitch climbs the right dihedral (left facing) up to a small roof, which is turned on the right (crux). Head right just a little bit more and pick up a crack which is followed to an uncomfortable belay where the crack terminates at a horizontal fissure.

The third pitch continues up and slightly left to another crack and up to a small tree. From here, cut straight right over to the leftward rising roof band, and crank the roof at a crack with a pin in it. Keep going straight up towards Paperback Ledge, and turn a final roof (orange/red colored). A few more feet puts you on the ledge itself.

Cottontail (5.6) starts up a very long left facing flake/corner system to the left and uphill of **The Dog**. A long pitch of 5.5 ends at a ledge which comprises the bottom part of a mouth-shaped feature. Belay.

The second pitch heads up and left out of the mouth to a crack which is followed up into a large right facing dihedral. Follow this as it arches to the right, then pick up the final 5.4 crack and head to the ledge.

Zingando (5.5) is the easiest and shortest route on the Left Book. Uphill from **Cottontail** is a huge arch-shaped impression. Scramble up the slab which leads up to a big left facing flake/corner, and ascend it up to a crack which in turn is followed up to a roof. Step left a little and turn the roof (crux), then continue up to a nice belay at a tree.

Head up, then break out right at a rising hand crack (5.4). Pick up the last few feet of **Cottontail** near Paperback Ledge.

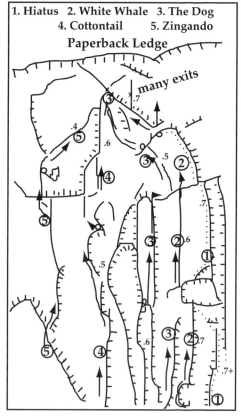

1. Hiatus   2. White Whale   3. The Dog
4. Cottontail   5. Zingando
Paperback Ledge
many exits

The Bookend

The Bookend is the furthest west crag in the Book group. The Bookend is instantly recognizable by its arrowhead shape and distinctive large flakes and chimneys on the south face. Just like the Left Book and the Bookmark, the Bookend is under-visited. Great climbing abounds here and you'll probably never have to wait for a route.

On the southeast side of the crag, a broad slab (third class) stretches across the base. The first two routes require a quick scramble up this slab to a grassy ledge. Another marking feature of the Bookend is a compact mini-buttress called The Foxhead that sits on the southwest corner of the Bookend.

Approach the Bookend by taking the Book trail off the Black Canyon Trail. Bear left at the sign for the Bookmark, but continue walking west below the Bookmark until you come to the base of the Bookend.

Descend from the summit by heading north to easy ground, then turn east and pick up a convenient gully to the base.

Sorcerer (5.9) begins on the grassy ledge below a nice left facing corner system that runs nearly all the way to the summit. Climb the corner (5.6) to an alcove, then continue to the right with a nice flake (5.8) and belay at a stance even with a roof to the left. The next pitch, a long and thinly protected one, climbs the corner directly above to a belay below another flake/roof.

Continue with the corner. Where it heads sharply left (forming another roof), make a choice. (1) Turn the roof right where it forms (5.7) and continue up the 5.6 flake above to the summit. (2) Continue out left below the roof and turn it at its left terminus (5.8). Belay. The last pitch continues up over easier ground to the summit.

Climb of the Ancient Mariner (5.10a) is an ever-popular Bookend route that climbs the clean slab just left of **Sorcerer**. Begin with the first 50 feet of **Sorcerer**, but break out left to a right facing corner when the alcove is reached. Ascend the corner to the roof above, turn it on the left (protected by a bolt), then continue up the slab (10a) past two more bolts to a two bolt belay.

The second pitch climbs straight up past six more bolts (5.9 and *very* runout at times), then heads left to the edge of the last roof on **Sorcerer** and finish on that route.

Labor of Lust (5.10c R) climbs the beautiful rounded prow left of Mariner. Begin up two parallel flared cracks and head to a stance with a bolt (5.7).

Pitch two —the crux— ascends the prow past three old bolts. (Look for gear placements in a short dihedral out left at mid-height). Belay in a corner.

The final pitch continues on the arete past a bolt, then climbs a roof via a finger crack.

Handbook (5.9) is another fine line that follows the crack and corner system left of Lust. Start from a grassy ledge right of Orange Julius. The first pitch climbs a wide crack to a sloping belay (5.7, 70').

Pitch two ascends the steep left facing corner for 120'. Belay at a good stance (5.9).

The final pitch switches over to a crack on the right and eventually joins Sorcerer (5.6).

The Great Dihedral (5.7) isn't a bad route if you don't mind chimneys. Begin from the grassy ledges and follow the large dihedral/chimney that separates the crag into north and south features.

Hot Licks (5.9+) is solid for its grade. Be ready to climb a 5.9 offwidth and bring many large Friends. Begin up **Great Dihedral**, but head left into a hand crack just a short ways off the deck. Ascend the crack and belay after 100 feet or so (wherever comfortable).

The second pitch follows the crack until it dies. Where it does, continue up and right over 5.8+ face to another crack. Follow this as it heads right some more, then straight up to a belay on a small ledge.

The final pitch heads right into the plain-as-day offwidth, and follows this (stout 5.9) to its top. Belay.

Easy ground leads to the summit.

Orange Julius (5.9) is another Bookend favorite. Begin below the very large triangular roof. Ascend a steep flared crack created by a small pillar, then head left where a dihedral begins, and climb into a small crack. Continue over unprotected 5.9 face to the left edge of the roof above, and continue up to a belay at a tree. A variation continues up the corner (instead of heading left at the thin crack) to the roof, then underclings left under the roof (l0b), heading up at its end to the same belay tree. Better protection exists on the harder variation.

The second pitch heads up the crack above, then heads up and right across slabby ground when it ends. Pick up another crack, and climb straight up to a belay beneath a big orange alcove.

Next, traverse right over grim 5.8+ friction and pick up the jagged crack on the second pitch of **Hot Licks**. Climb the crack to the same small ledge belay.

The fourth pitch heads left via an amazing 5.7 hand traverse. Belay at the end of the crack.

The next pitch climbs the 5.8 crack above, then cuts left and joins the chimney for the last few feet. Easy ground then leads to the summit.

The Bookend

1. Sorcerer 5.8+
2. Climb of the Ancient Mariner 5.10a
3. Labor of Lust 5.10c R
4. Handbook 5.9

5. The Great Dihedral 5.7
6. Hot Licks 5.9
7. Orange Julius 5.9
8. Sun King 5.11b

Sun King (5.11b) begins halfway between the Foxhead on the right and a deep chimney on the left. Climb via cracks to the first bolt. Follow the line as it meanders past three more bolts (no move harder than 5.10d). After the last bolt, head left to a compact left-facing flake and lieback it to a two bolt belay.

The second pitch heads up and left to the roof/bulge above, then follows a line of four more bolts to a bolt belay.

Descend by rappelling 85 feet to the first belay, then another 85 feet to a point 15 feet off the ground. Downclimb the rest, or better yet, use a 60 meter rope.

Lens Rock

Lens Rock is a good destination on Lumpy Ridge for climbers of any ability. It is an aptly named crag as the easternmost section sports a large, smooth slab, shaped like a lens. The western side is also a clean and pretty slab, but it is lower angled, and is split by two distinct intersecting cracks. The two halves of Lens Rock are split by a long chimney (**Right Chimney**).

Approach Lens Rock by utilizing the Book approach, then head off toward the Bookend. Stay high and keep heading west until it comes into view.

To descend from the summit, head east off the top, then bear south where a gully permits. The rest of the descent to the south is somewhat nebulous. Various jogs east are required to allow a rappel-free descent.

The Frame (5.8+) is the offwidth on the far right side of the lens slab. It is a beautiful, clean crack, and makes a good training climb for those aspiring to **Crack of Fear**. Follow the crack up to the top of the lens.

Ellipse (5.12a) ascends a bolt line straight up the middle of the lens. Get to the base of the route by ascending a 5.5 groove/ chimney below the left side of the lens. Don't make the mistake of using **Right Chimney** for the approach.

Begin the route by mounting the lens directly below two bolts. This is the crux. Continue up into a shallow seam (RPs), then follow six more bolts up to a two bolt anchor.

Arch Crack (5.6) begins up **Right Chimney** and climbs until a move left gets one into the left-arching crack that cuts across the left side of Lens Rock. Break off and head straight up where it intersects a vertical crack. At a ledge, heading right leads to the descent slabs. If you opt to climb the flake/corner straight up to the top, it's 5.7.

Tennis Shoe Tango (5.6) starts up a chimney which lies on the far left side of the crag next to the big dihedral. Climb the 5.5 chimney, head right along a horizontal weakness, and belay below the vertical crack.

The second pitch climbs the crack all the way to the ledge. Pick a finish.

Lens Rock

1. The Frame 5.8+   2. Ellipse 5.12a
3. Arch Crack 5.6   4. Tennis Shoe Tango 5.6

The Pear

The Pear is a large, broad crag that lies just west of Lens Rock. It is a favorite destination for moderate leaders, but it also sports many fine routes of greater difficulty. From the south the Pear is unmistakable as it rises to a small rounded summit.

The Pear is approached via the Black Canyon Trail. Follow the trail for a little over a mile. Pass through a big swinging gate, then bear right onto a narrow trail marked by a sign. This approach trail meanders through boulders and winds up just below and to the left of the huge dihedral that splits the lower half of the Pear.

Descend from the summit by making a long single rope rappel to the north into a neat corridor. Down the shoulder to the east of the summit are more bolts and chains. One of the routes in this guide is actually a toprope in the corridor beneath these shoulder chains, which can be reached from the summit by easy scrambling. Walk west to exit the corridor (it's much easier to get back to your gear), and descend the gully to the south.

Fat Bottomed Groove (5.10d) is a good burly test for Pear climbers. Begin below the right edge of the big roof band which cuts across the middle third of the Pear near the ground. Climb the 5.8 chimney up to the roof band, or take a 10c crack just right of the chimney to the same place. Enjoy unusual traversing to the left (crux) and crank the roof at a flake with slings around it. Belay just above the roof.

The second pitch heads straight up a white pillar (small pro, 5.9), then heads left at its top to a belay on lower angled terrain.

The next pitch traverses easy 5.0 ground right for quite a ways until a nice walk off ledge is encountered on the southeast side of the Pear.

The Whole Thing **(5.10a)** begins left of **Fat Bottomed Groove** and ascends broken third class terrain to a tree on a ledge. Head straight up a crack, then up and left to a single bolt before encountering the roof. Turn the roof (crux) at an indentation (protected by two bolts), then climb into a short left facing flake and belay at its top.

The next pitch heads straight out left across an unprotected slab to a thin crack which is followed up (5.9+) to a left facing corner. Head up this to the easy traverse and the walk off ledge mentioned in **Fat Bottomed Groove**.

Sibling Rivalry (5.9+) begins at the far right end of the roof band where the roof itself is stepped. Climb up into any of the thin cracks or flakes (5.8 runout on the left, 5.7 runout on the right) which head up to the roof (runout again). Clip a bolt beneath the roof, turn the thing, then belay in the 5.7 crack just above.

Head left to the arête formed by the huge dihedral and cruise up exquisite rock past four bolts to a two bolt anchor. Belay. Rappel 165 feet to the ground.

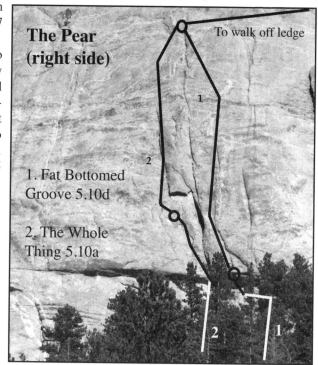

The Pear
(right side)

To walk off ledge

1. Fat Bottomed Groove 5.10d

2. The Whole Thing 5.10a

Magical Chrome Plated Semi-Automatic Enema Syringe (5.6). What more can be said after a route name like that? This is another of Lumpy's mega-classic moderates, and should be added to anyone's "must do" list.

Begin by climbing a small broken buttress (third class) that lies below and left of the huge dihedral. At the top of the buttress, ascend the left crack (5.5) up to where an obvious leftward hand traverse can be made. The traverse goes at about 5.6, and protects well. Belay below the nice clean dihedral at the end of the traverse.

Make a funky move over the corner/roof, and lieback the corner all the way to its top, fantastic 5.6. Belay on the huge ledge.

Climb up the left side of the broken flake to a ramp which leads up towards the summit block. Belay at a small tree growing out of the crack along the ramp.

The fourth pitch continues for a short distance up the ramp, then breaks right into a nice crack (5.6) which heads straight up the slab beneath the summit block. There are a couple of steep sections, but nothing too difficult. Belay beneath the summit block on another nice ledge.

The final pitch follows one of three lines. Either traverse right beneath the summit to a tricky 5.7 right facing corner which leads to the top. Attack the overhanging 5.9 fist crack on the block, or traverse around to the left and climb broken 5.7 terrain to the top.

La Chaim (5.7) is a quality 5.7, but it's a little runout at the bottom. Begin to the left of the broken buttress used on **Magical...** and climb via 5.5 face (not much pro) to a ledge with a tree. Continue up to the top of a left facing flake and belay beneath the crack above.

The second pitch heads up the crack (crux, bring lots of small stoppers) to the big walk off ledge.

Jam On It (5.9) is the beautiful handcrack below and to the left of the shoulder rap anchors. The route can certainly be led, but most parties opt for the quick toprope. Do it on your way out.

The Pear (Left Side)

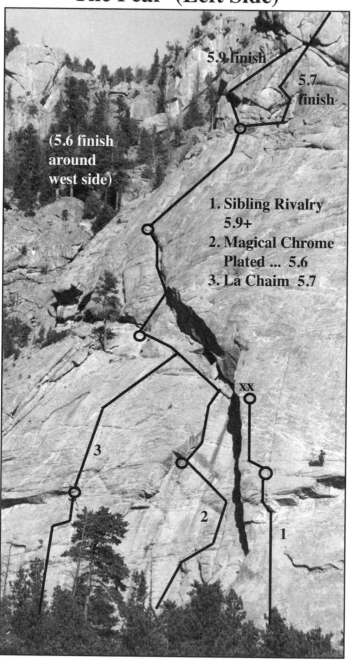

5.9 finish

5.7 finish

(5.6 finish around west side)

1. Sibling Rivalry 5.9+
2. Magical Chrome Plated ... 5.6
3. La Chaim 5.7

XX

3

2

1

Sundance Buttress

Sundance Buttress certainly isn't the most visited rock on Lumpy Ridge, but it is far and away the most majestic. Sundance stands guard at the west end of the ridge, and towers 700 to 800 feet off the valley floor. There are many days during the climbing season when you may be the only party on Sundance. The long approach (over 2 miles, and a little steep at the end) seems to deter most parties, but don't fall prey to this thinking.

The rock is super clean, and the buttress itself is massive—from the parking lot and all along the Black Canyon Trail, the only section of the Sundance the climber sees is the rounded wall of Turnkorner Buttress. As you continue along the trail below Sundance it unravels to the west, revealing an incredible amount of fantastic rock.

Sundance is split into four areas. They are, from east to west: the Northeast Slabs (comprising the easternmost wall), Turnkorner Buttress (mentioned previously), the Guillotine Wall (named for an old route of the same name), and the Eumenides Slab (bordered on the east by the massive Eumenides Dihedral).

Descend from the summit of Sundance by heading into the saddle between the summit of Turnkorner and the true summit of Sundance. Head northeast down a series of ledges and slabs. This is a solid fourth class downclimb. We recommend rappelling from any of the trees which abound in this area. A couple of double rope rappels put you at the top of an easy descent gully which heads south to the base of the rock.

The Nose

The Nose (5.10b) is one of Sundance's coveted routes. Just like its more famous relative of the same name (somewhere in California, I hear), it follows the distinct "nose" of Turnkorner Buttress from base to summit.

Begin up a gully bordered on the right by a big left facing corner, climb up to a flake, then bear left and climb into the right side of a distinct pillar. Ascend the crack (5.9) in the pillar to the top and belay.

Next, climb up into a right facing flake. At its top, friction to the left and enter a big crack. Climb to the top and belay at two bolts.

The third pitch climbs the crack above the belay, then heads left until under the very left edge of the big roof. Cruise up then head left out of a small dihedral. Scary face climbing back to the right (5.9+) leads to a belay directly beneath the left edge of the roof. Avoid the temptation to follow the bolts out left.

Now head right and turn the roof at a weakness which cuts back left (5.10b). Where the crack dies, face climb right (5.8, no pro) into a crack and belay at a piton and a bolt.

Follow the deep groove up to the right edge of the next big roof above. Make a quick 5.8 move right and leave the roof behind. Belay at the end of the groove.

Follow easy low angled rock for a couple more pitches to the top of Turnkorner.

Turnkorner (5.10b) is a favorite among Lumpy climbers, and is highly recommended.

Begin the route a ways to the left of **The Nose** near a big reclining flake. On the left side of the flake is a big corner. Ascend this (5.9) obtuse feature and belay atop it.

Pick the left crack and jam it (more 5.9) to a belay stance on small ledge with boulders.

Head up yet another 5.9 crack which arches slightly left, then follow the ramp left past a bolt (not the newest bolt, to be sure) and take the difficult overhanging fist crack (10b) off the left edge. Continue up the wide crack above past more antique bolts (5.9) and belay in slings below the imposing roof above.

Next, head straight up into the roof, and struggle through it via an offwidth 10a crack. Guaranteed, this will feel at least as hard as the overhanging fist crack below. Above is a 5.9 crack which is followed for a long ways to a belay at its top.

The grunting is over. Head right into a 5.6 crack and belay on a ledge which circles Turnkorner Buttress below the summit.

The next pitch heads left and up from the ledge and picks up a meandering 5.6 crack. Belay where the crack hits a small right facing corner.

Head to the top via low angled terrain.

Chain of Command (5.11a) begins about 120 feet to the left of **Turnkorner** below a hanging dihedral. Face climb up and left into the base of the dihedral via scary 5.9 face climbing. Ascend the corner (10a at the bottom, 10b at the top) and belay at two bolts. This first pitch is actually a route called **Bonzo**.

Now head up and slightly left to a bolt, clip that mother, and follow 10a face climbing past five more. At the last bolt, head straight right to a belay atop a flake at two bolts.

The short third pitch climbs up past two more bolts (crux) to another two bolt belay. Rappel the route (single rope is fine, but 60 meters is a better length).

Kor's Flake (5.7+) is the first route in this book on the very popular Guillotine Wall. Turnkorner and Guillotine are separated by a deep chimney system which runs all the way to the saddle. Hike west along the base of Sundance until the chimney is passed. Enter the next chimney encountered (about 50 feet past the large chimney) and climb it up to a groove. Follow this groove (5.6) up and right. Belay on a good ledge below a very large flake which leans up and left. Climb up into the flake (crux), and belay along its edge after about 100 feet.

Continue up the flake (the crack behind it widens as you climb) and belay atop a vertical flake that abuts it.

Friction left then up into a section of small broken corners. Continue up and left to a crack splitting a roof/bulge. Belay at the end of the crack at a pin (below a roof).

Pass the roof on the left side (5.7), then head to the saddle via easy terrain.

Mainliner (5.9) is among the finest 5.9s on the ridge. Begin about 200 feet left of the **Kor's Flake** chimney at an amazing (and obtuse) left facing corner. Climb this (5.8), break left at its end, and continue up an adjacent corner to a belay under a sharp left bend in the dihedral system

The next pitch heads up and left up a face into a nice crack, then over more face (5.8 or so) and into another crack, finally ending on a big ledge. Belay. Head straight up off the ledge into a crack which leads to a short section of opposing dihedrals. Stem up (5.9-) and enter another crack. Follow this to its end, then head right and belay on a small ledge at the base of a large left facing corner.

Climb the corner (5.7) to much easier terrain. Belay where comfortable.

Traverse right to reach the saddle and the descent route, or on to the summit (fairly easy).

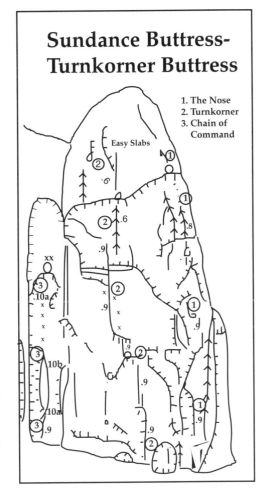

Sundance Buttress-
Turnkorner Buttress

1. The Nose
2. Turnkorner
3. Chain of Command

Easy Slabs

Sidetrack (5.9) begins in the next crack left of **Mainliner** that reaches the ground. Climb the crack (5.8) then face to a belay below the intersection of two corners which forms an indention.

The next pitch climbs the right facing corner, turns the roof on the left (5.9), and continues with the crack above. Belay at the base of a new crack after a short stretch of face.

Head up the crack (5.8) for a long pitch to a belay on a nice V-shaped ledge.

Next, follow the groove above (5.6) to another good ledge.

The fifth pitch steps right, then climbs the 5.9 crack into an awkward A-shaped roof. Pass the roof via hard stems and weird positions. Continue with the crack above and belay on lower angled ground.

Head up to the summit, or up then traverse right to the saddle.

Grapevine (5.8+) is an old Layton Kor route that begins 50 feet left of **Sidetrack** below an orange/yellow wall. Climb into a crack that doesn't quite reach the ground and veer right into a groove which climbs to the right of the orange plaque. Belay on a little pedestal at its end.

The next pitch climbs the 5.6 chimney straight off the belay. Where it dies, head left up a right facing flake/corner to a good ledge at its top.

Start up the crack off the ledge, but head right into an easier crack just ten feet or so from the ledge. Follow this nice 5.8 crack to a ledge at the bottom of a big left facing corner. Belay.

Climb the corner (crux) and belay 50 feet past its top. Cruise easier ground to the summit.

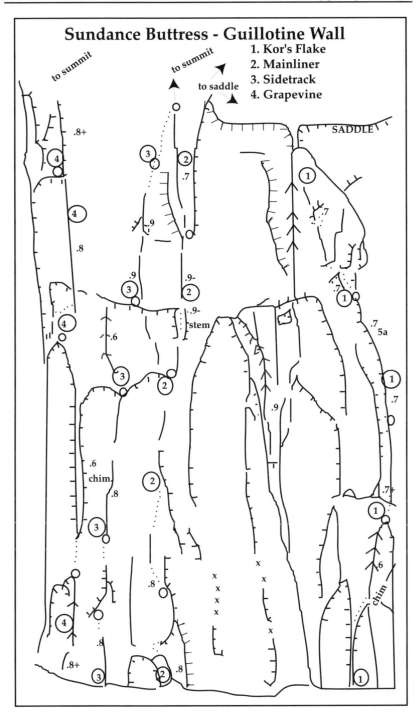

Sundance Buttress - Guillotine Wall

1. **Kor's Flake**
2. **Mainliner**
3. **Sidetrack**
4. **Grapevine**

The final route on Lumpy Ridge in this guide is on the Eumenides Slab. Walk beneath the face of Sundance, passing all the previous routes. The huge Eumenides dihedral is to the left of **Grapevine's** orange wall.

Eumenides (5.8) begins directly below its namesake dihedral. Climb third class rock up to the dihedral. It steepens near the bottom, so rope up if you need to. Ascend the dihedral for 150 feet (5.8), then cut left to a ledge. Belay.

Climb up the slab into a series of left facing corners, and continue for another 150 feet to a belay on a sloping ledge.

The third pitch has plenty of excitement. Head left off the ledge and climb a short crack, followed by face up and left to another short crack. Finish this crack, then head up and right to yet short crack. Belay at its top.

Friction right, then head up and left, aiming for the bottom of the big left facing corner above. Belay at its base.

Climb the corner to a roof, turn it on either side (both 5.8), and go to the summit.. An intermediate belay may be necessary.

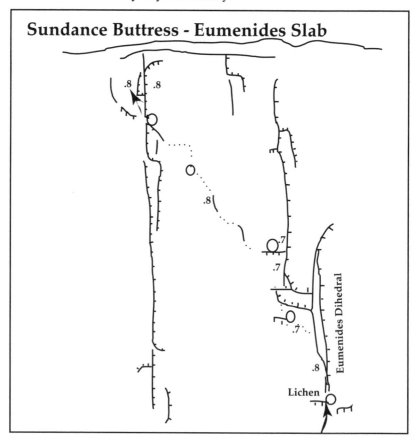

Sundance Buttress - Eumenides Slab

.8   .8

.8

.7

.7

.7

Eumenides Dihedral

.8

Lichen

ESTES AREA
CRAGS

Michelle Hurni at Prospect Mountain
Dan Hare photo

PROSPECT MOUNTAIN

Prospect Mountain, a small crag south of Estes Park, provides a great crag for days of iffy weather. Most of the routes are topropes or sport climbs. The Thumb and the Needle are the most prominent rocks rising from the eastern flank of Prospect Mountain, and contain most of the good climbing.

To reach this area take Highway 7 to Peak View Drive. Continue 1.0 miles to a dirt road (making sure not to fork right on Devon Road). Follow the dirt road for 0.7 miles to a pull-out before a gate. Look for a foot trail rather than hiking up the wide gully. A short 5-minute walk leads to the cliffs.

Topropes will be addressed separately from lead climbs. For more information on toproping in the Estes Park region, consult *FRONT RANGE TOPROPES* by Fred Knapp.

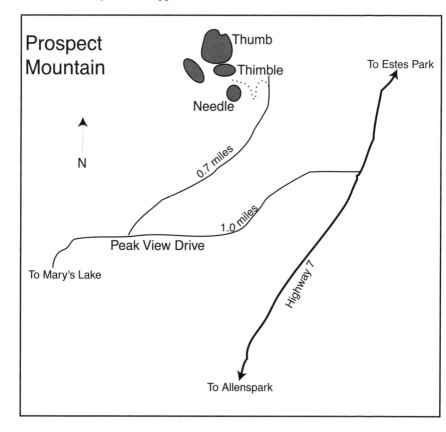

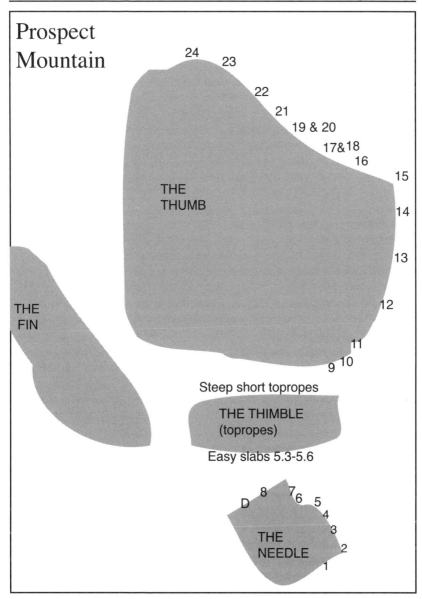

Prospect Mountain

THE THUMB

THE FIN

Steep short topropes

THE THIMBLE (topropes)

Easy slabs 5.3-5.6

THE NEEDLE

1. Angels Overhang (5.11) A toprope problem that climbs over roofs near the arete left of Suburban Hangover.

2. Suburban Hangover (5.11a) Stick-clip the first bolt of this powerful climb which ascends both sides of the arete.

3. Momentary Lapse of Ethics (5.11a or 5.12a) This route splits near the top to offer a 5.11 or a rather contrived 5.12 finish. Begins right of #2.

4. Temple of the Dog (5.13a) Begin beneath a left-facing corner to the right of the previous route. Climb through the most difficult section of rock on the wall.

5. And the Damage Done (5.11b) The area classic. Powerful moves lead out a steep roof. The route wanders to the right side of the wall where technical footwork kicks in. 5 bolts.

6. North Lieback (5.10a trad) The obvious lieback through a left-facing dihedral.

7. Bustin' Move (5.12b) A series of left-angling roofs create road blocks. Bust a big move at the third bolt.

8. Uphill Slab (5.8R) Rarely led but often toproped, this route climbs a steep slab past two dysfunctional bolts.

D. Descent Route (4th class) An easy endeavor but routefinding is quite difficult.

9. Toprope (5.7) Toprope this from the chain anchors.

10. Toprope (5.7) Ditto for #9.

11. Passage to Anchors (5.4) A system of broken corners lead to the toprope anchors.

11a. Left Center (5.8+ R) Rarely climbed, this route takes a line that corresponds to the orange lichen streak. Not shown on overview. Oops.

12. Pin Job (5.10b) This line, which is a bit loose and scary, begins right of a 10-foot pillar. Climb a short dihedral to a descent anchor then continue past fixed pins to a bolted belay. A 60 meter rope is required for a single lower from this station.

13. Right Center (5.7R) From the rappel anchor on Pin Job head right into dihedrals following occasional fixed hardware and a belay beneath a black groove. Continue up the groove (5.6) to the top.

14. Northeast Chimney (5.8) Begin up the obvious chimney and belay at a ledge with two pins. Join the black groove of the previous route to finish the route.

15. Grey Arete (5.10X) The steep grey lichened arete. Scary.

16. Zig Arete (5.10d) This is the escape from the scary end of Grey Arete. Move left after the 4th bolt.

17. Confines of Power (5.12a) Seven bolts protect this stellar line.

18. Vapor Trail (5.12d) This is the right-hand variation to Confines of Power. Also bolted.

19. North Overhang (5.9) Follows the huge left-facing dihedral in the middle of the north face. Sneak around the upper roof to the right.

20. Mind Over Matter (5.12a) Approach this huge roof via North Overhang. Totally trad. Taking the right branch of the roof crack is easier (5.11c) and is dubbed **Never Mind, It Doesn't Matter.**

21. Pigeon Perch (5.9R) Begin as for North Roof but head left at the sloping shelf past a single bolt to a bolt anchor.

22. North Roof (5.10c) Begin with a left-facing dihedral and jam a wide crack through the roof.

23. Uphill Cracks (5.7) start west of the previous routes.

24. A Reason to Bolt (5.9+R) Begin below some orange lichen. Follow bolts and pins. The first moves are sketchy.

HIGH PEAKS

Ron Crotzer on Stettner's Ledges
Gary Neptune photo

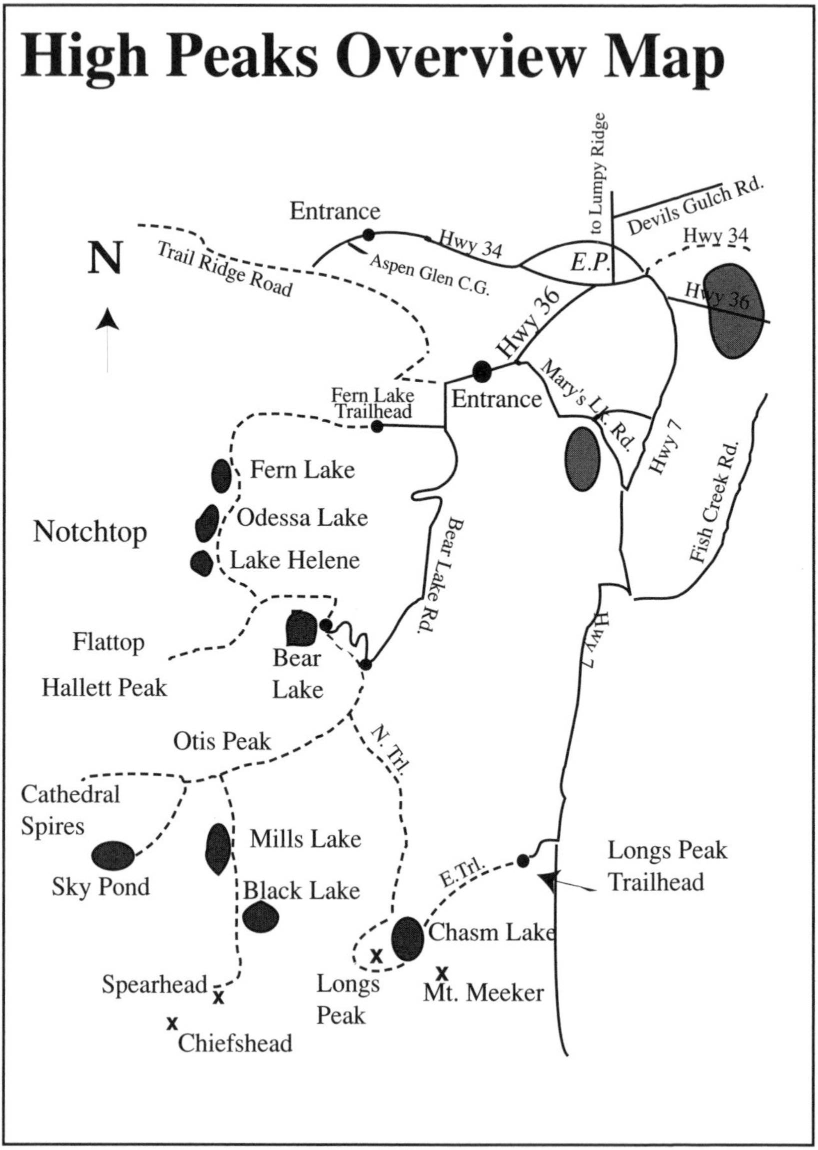

High Peaks Overview Map

to Lumpy Ridge

Devils Gulch Rd.

Entrance

Hwy 34

Aspen Glen C.G.

Trail Ridge Road

Hwy 34

E.P.

Hwy 36

N

Hwy 36

Fern Lake
Trailhead

Entrance

Mary's Lk. Rd.

Hwy 7

Fern Lake

Fish Creek Rd.

Notchtop

Odessa Lake

Lake Helene

Bear Lake Rd.

Flattop

Bear

Hallett Peak

Lake

Otis Peak

N. Trl.

Cathedral
Spires

Mills Lake

Hwy 7

Sky Pond

Black Lake

E. Trl.

Longs Peak
Trailhead

Chasm Lake

Spearhead x

x

Longs
Peak

x
Mt. Meeker

x
Chiefshead

THE HIGH PEAKS

While Lumpy Ridge holds the majority of routes in the park, the high peaks are the undisputed heart and soul of climbing in Rocky Mountain National Park. A climbing trip to the park just isn't complete without doing at least one of the routes listed on the following pages.

Among the high peaks are some of the most classic and sought after walls and lines in the United States. Steck and Roper's book *50 Classic Climbs of North America* includes three routes from the park. While these routes are often crowded (especially the South Face of the Petit Grepon), all of the other climbs detailed in this book are worthy of inclusion on anyone's "best of" list.

Longs Peak, Hallett Peak, Petit Grepon, Notchtop, Spearhead Chiefshead...the impressive list goes on. One can hardly go wrong when choosing a high country route. To make sure the climb is enjoyable, remember to follow the advice in *ALPINE ROCK 101* in the introduction to this guide.

If you're planning on bivying in the Park you must have a backcountry permit. Although permits are available to "walk-ins" calling ahead for reservations is a better option. Summer reservations may be made in May. An administration fee of $15 per person allows you up to seven nights in the backcountry. Call the office at 970-586-1242 between 8:00 and 4:30 for more information.

PACK OUT EVERY SINGLE ITEM YOU BROUGHT IN WITH YOU. ABSOLUTELY, POSITIVELY NO EXCUSES ON THIS ONE. LEAVE THE PARK AS YOU FOUND IT - CLEAN AND PRISTINE.

NATIONAL PARK INFORMATION

Visitor Center Hours:
9am to 5pm daily

Cost of Entry:
$10 per private vehicle

Main Phone Number:
(weather, recording, other #'s)
970-586-1333

Campsite Reservations:
1-800-365-2267

Backcountry Office:
970-586-1242

GLACIER GORGE

For scenic beauty, rock quality, and abundance of excellent routes, Glacier Gorge might be the highlight of the high peaks of Rocky Mountain National Park. Spearhead and Chiefshead are set in a cirque formed by Longs Peak, Pagoda Peak, and McHenry's Peak. Unlike the Diamond or Hallett Peak, the routes on Chiefshead and Spearhead don't overlook the eastern plains.

The approach to the Glacier Gorge cirque is rather lengthy but is generally flat and easygoing. Begin at the Glacier Gorge Parking lot and hike the main trail to a junction a ways past Alberta Falls. At this point, follow the trail to Black Lake and Glacier Gorge, rather than the right-hand alternative to Loch Vale. Hike past Mills Lake (2.5 miles), continue to Black Lake (about 5 miles), then continue on a more primitive trail that leads to the slabby and wet opening of Glacier Gorge. Follow cairns through these slabs, then continue through the tundra to the Spearhead. To approach the Northwest Face of Chiefshead, continue around the right side of Spearhead and hike through talus to the base. To approach the Northeast Face, continue around the left side of Spearhead.

Spearhead (12,578)

Spearhead is another of the park's aptly named peaks. This stunning feature juts up from the tundra of upper Glacier Gorge. Spearhead's northeast face is massive and rises some 800 feet from the base to the broken summit block. The rock is high quality granite, and many beautiful natural lines exist.

Spearhead sports a couple of features which help in route finding. The first is the big ledge which cuts across the entire face about 1/4 of the way up. This is called Middle Earth Ledge. The other feature is the Eye of Mordor, which is a depressed feature in the rock shaped like a vertical eye. It lies a little above Middle Earth and on the left half of the face. It's hard to miss.

Ascending the summit block of Spearhead can be tricky. There are many options, but we recommend locating a small chimney/hole, which can be wriggled up to reach the summit. The hole drops out onto the northeast face and would present a climber with an awfully long fall, so rope up when heading to the top.

Many climbers choose to bivy at the base of Spearhead (be sure to get a permit from the backcountry office), but all of the routes can be completed in a day from car to car.

The most direct, albeit tedious, descent is to scramble down the eternal scree of the west slopes. A semi-trail down one of the gullies should be somewhat obvious if one doesn't go too far north.

North Ridge (III, 5.6) is perhaps the best moderate route in the high country. The climbing is exposed and entertaining, and the rock quality is about as good as it gets.

The route begins on the slabs at the base of the ridge (the right skyline when viewed from the northeast) and continues through a steep chimney at about 80 feet (5.5). Belay at a good stance nearly a rope length up, or break the pitch beneath the second step of the chimney.

Several easy pitches follow slabs and cracks until the rock steepens several hundred feet higher. Many variations exist through this section.

From here the route tends to the left towards the arete, where the climber gets a taste of big exposure as she peers down the expansive northeast face. A left-facing dihedral pitch offers the best, most exposed, and easiest passage through this section. Several other options exist to the right, though lichen and thinner cracks increase the difficulty.

Another dihedral, also very exposed, leads one to easy scrambling and, ultimately, the summit register.

The Barb (III, 5.10c) ascends a zig-zag crack system on the right side of the Barb — the detached looking barb-ish thing on the right side of the Northeast Face. The route starts up a left facing corner on the far right side of the lower face and belays at a ledge (5.7).

Another easy (5.4) pitch gains Middle Earth ledge.

Walk left along this ledge for 100 feet or so, then climb an easy section of rock for about half a rope length and belay below and to the right of an obvious right facing corner.

The next pitch climbs up into the corner and follows it to its top. Belay.

Now ascend a thin left-leaning 5.9 crack with tricky pro at the start. Belay beneath an overhang.

The next pitch cranks the A-shaped roof, ascends the crack above, and belays at a miserable stance in a left-facing corner (5.9).

Ascend the corner for a hundred feet (5.9). Next, a shuffle down and left to a crack which ends just beneath the Barb flake. Several 5.10 moves gain access to the flake which is climbed to its terminus at the North Ridge. Follow the last two pitches of the North Ridge to the summit.

Bret Ruckman on Spear Me the Details
Jack Roberts photo; Ruckman collection

Descend by the standard descent or one may continue down a gully system down the east (left as one faces the wall) side of Spearhead. Essentially this is a scramble down a large slabular corner system. This method avoids the terminal talus and returns you to your pack via the most direct path.

Sykes Sickle (III, 5.9+) was the first route up the northeast face, and for that reason alone is considered a classic. It climbs straight up into the big arching dihedral (the Sickle) that dominates the upper half of the face.

Start up the center of the face in a left-facing corner, just left of another crack (5.7). Belay at the top of the corner. A 5.4 pitch wanders to Middle Earth.

Two 5.5-5.6 pitches wander up and slightly right along good edges and ledges to a belay beneath a wide right facing corner system.

Climb the corner (5.7) and belay at its top (even with the bottom of the Sickle).

Ascend the chimney up the left side of the sickle, or take the cracks out right, 5.7 either way. Belay on a good little ledge directly below a notch in the ominous roof of the Sickle.

The next pitch is the crux (stiff 5.9) and cranks the roof through the notch (protected by pins), then continues via a 5.7 crack to a belay at a flake.

Continue up and right over a runout 5.7 slab past a piton and a bolt and finish on the ledge below the summit block.

Spear Me the Details (III, 5.11c/d) The name of this route has to do with the bolting method of the first ascenscionists. The route puts together much interesting terrain and offers two excellent 5.11 pitches.

Start on the left side of the lower wall and angle up slabs on very easy terrain to attain the Middle Earth Ledge. The real climbing starts beneath the Eye of Mordor. Follow face holds and incipient cracks to a belay at a ledge (5.8).

A very long pitch (simul-climbing is required if you do not have a 60 meter rope) takes one to a belay at the left side of an obvious pillar (5.7).

The next pitch ascends the wide left facing corner of the pillar (5.8).

A moderately loose face pitch climbs past a couple of pins and a bolt to a belay stance beneath a roof. Several belay possibilities exist for this 10b pitch.

At the smallest part of the roof, clip a bolt and do a mid-5.10 mantle to a belay in a corner beneath the roof.

The next pitch is the crux. Climb over the roof, avoiding the temptation to ascend the crack straight-on. Follow three bolts and a pin to a difficult mantle move which gains a guillotine-esque flake (I thought this was the crux). Four more bolts protect difficult face climbing (the first-ascensionists thought this was the crux) to an uncomfortable belay at the base of a corner.

Climb the corner past bolts and a piton until it ends, move right into another corner which terminates at a very good belay ledge.

From here one can climb the corner to the right, then traverse down and left to another corner (5.9+) or one can continue , more or less straight up, past a bolt into a crack (5.10). Either finish requires careful protection, so that both the leader and follower remain safe. Descend the same way as for **The Barb.**.

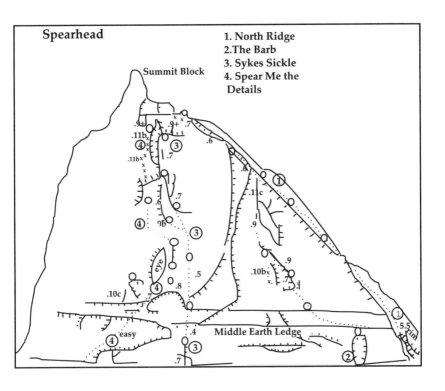

Spearhead

Summit Block

1. North Ridge
2. The Barb
3. Sykes Sickle
4. Spear Me the Details

Middle Earth Ledge

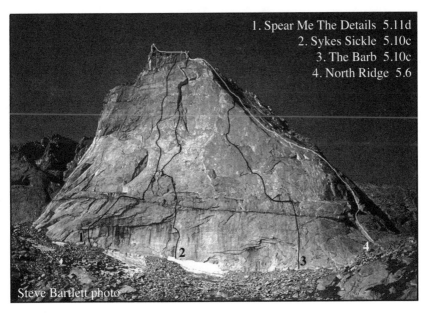

1. Spear Me The Details 5.11d
2. Sykes Sickle 5.10c
3. The Barb 5.10c
4. North Ridge 5.6

Steve Bartlett photo

Chiefshead (13,579')

Chiefshead is the peak located behind Spearhead when viewed during the approach. Its north face appears less as a dramatic peak and more as a mile-long ridge of rock about 1,000 feet high. A prominent buttress divides the north face and essentially terminates at a junction with Spearhead. The face to the right as viewed during the approach is considered the northwest face and the eastern left-hand wall is the northeast face.

Approach Chiefshead via the Spearhead approach. To approach the NW face, continue around the west side of Spearhead.

The **Birds of Fire** (5.10d) route on Chiefshead holds significant importance to the climbing community, as well as to me personally. In 1988, when rappel bolting was extremely controversial, Richard Rossiter made a very bold statement by placing many of "Birds of Fire's" bolts while hanging from a rope. Much of the climbing community was up in arms, for not only was **Birds** the first rap bolted route of the high country, but it was on Chiefshead — a peak that boasted the boldest routes in the park. In 1961, Layton Kor and Bob Culp made the first ascent of the Northwest Face via an exceptionally bold 5.9. Charlie Fowler, accompanied by Dan McGee and John Harlin, added two more desperates in the 1980's — routes that hardly ever saw repeats due to their run-out nature and lack of retreat possibilities.

When word got around that a power drill was used, matters got even worse. Many climbers threatened to chop the route; I saw one climber moved to tears by what he saw as a violation of the sacredness of the mountains, and I even heard a few threats of physical harm to the first ascensionist. But the route remained, and as it began to see repeats, word of its quality spread. "It's by no means a sport route; it's still pretty run-out," was the common assessment. "It is spectacular," was a recurring appraisal. Still, I was unwilling to climb the route for many years, as I was strongly opposed to top-down tactics in the mountains.

Finally, at the end of the summer of 1992, I broke down and climbed the route. My partner was an athletic woman with little climbing experience in the big mountains. I had met her only once, but she was excited to do the route, and I was craving the high peaks. I had broken my arm in a motorcycle accident that summer, and had just had the cast removed that week. We made plans and a week later found ourselves at the parking lot at 4 a.m. —the wrong parking lot, unfortunately. The euphoria of climbing sans plaster, of being in the mountains, and of having a beautiful female companion, caused me to park at the upper lot, adding about 11/2 miles to the round trip journey.

We hiked in at a liesurely pace and found a party ahead of us. The snowfield was exceptionally large that year, and very icey that morning. When I was about halfway up the snow, I asked my companion if she'd be more comfortable with a rope. She declined. I knew that she had been on the U.S. ski team, so I reassured myself that she was plenty comfortable on snow. The suncupped glacier turned icier at the top, and where I made a large step between stances, my partner slipped. I watched as she slid head-first toward the talus. In the last ten feet, she managed to turn sideways and made contact with the talus with the side of her body. Bruised, bleeding, a little shaken, and belayed, she returned to my stance at the base.

Undaunted, we decided to continue the route. All went well until about the sixth pitch when it began to rain. We retreated, happy to have completed all but the last real pitch. After hiking through the talus, we decided to run the remaining six miles. And thus began a love affair.

Like all my loves, apart from mountains and canyons and wilderness, this ended. Chiefshead, however, is now perhaps a bit more special. So when I make the bold statement that "Birds of Fire" is my favorite route in Rocky Mountain Park, perhaps my judgement is clouded by circumstance more fluid and less objective than mere rock.

Birds of Fire (IV, 5.10d, R-) Ascend the snowfield to a giant flake shaped like my home state, Louisiana. Climb out right past a couple of bolts (5.9), over a roof protected by friends (5.10), past three more bolts to a ledge with a pin (RP's and funky gear can back up the pin). Several belay options exist: Belay from friends under the roof at 90'; or continue to the small ledge with the pin and belay there; or continue to the bolt and set up a belay there.

Continue left along the ledge to a bolted belay stance on a pedestal (a rope length above the roof). 5.10b.

Ascend the wall above the belay past two bolts (5.10d), proceed past another, then run it out on easier terrain to a bolted belay (140').

Another face pitch (10c) leads past a pin and some bolts, but also requires some unprotected climbing. A curving ramp leads to a belay beneath the prominent water streak.

The water streak offers excellent Toulumne-esque climbing on perfect rock with adequate protection. Five stars. Belay at bolts after 150' (5.9+).

Two bolts and a fixed pin takes one to another bolted stance (5.9, 150').

Climb left on flakes and edges to the base of a large dihedral (5.7, 75')

Climb the new bolted finish on the left arete of the gross dihedral (5.10b). Eventually head to the right over a small roof and belay at a ledge a full rope-length up.

Another 50' of climbing lead to bolt anchors (5.6).

Most people rappel the route, but one could continue to a large ledge system where one can hike west (right) then down a descent gully west of the cliff.

The Center Route (IV, 5.9+) is the first route up the wall, and was a hallmark route for its day (1961). The route could conceivably ascend any part of the wall right of **Birds of Fire**, and various descriptions have appeared over the years. Bob Culp drew me a topo of where he and Layton Kor had climbed, and it differs greatly from what has appeared in various climbing guidebooks. Perhaps this is because the wall is rarely as dry as when the route saw its pioneer ascent. The description I provide is one of the original line, which was incredibly unprotected, and involved simul-climbing to reach belay points (bring a long rope). TCUs and RPs will provide some protection, although not great!

Ascend a right-facing corner ramp to its top.

Corners and incipient cracks lead to a small ledge with an inadequate belay (5.9+).

A long face pitch climbs the black streak or the area around it to a belay corner (5.9 and dangerous). From **Birds of Fire** I saw an old bolt with a hanger made from a piton that Culp vaguely remembers as being theirs.

Continue up the easy corner to a belay.

A long RP and TCU protected 5.9 pitch climbs out right past a ledge to another ledge up and slightly right.

A 5.8 pitch climbs up a series of right-facing corners.

An unprotected 5.9+ traverse gains incipient cracks which provide another long pitch. Easier ground leads up to the top..

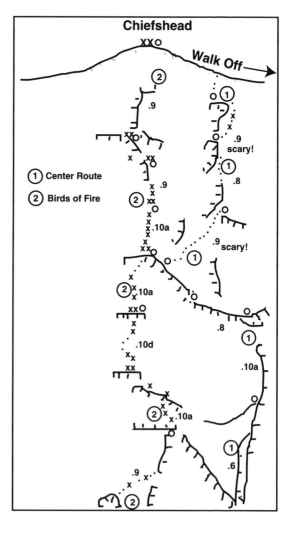

Chip Wilson on Birds of Fire   Steve "Crusher" Batrlett photo

Photo by Daniel Levison

Chiefshead

1. Center Route (aka Path of Elders) 5.10a R
2. Birds of Fire 5.10d

CATHEDRAL SPIRES

The Cathedral Spires houses perhaps the most sought after technical summit in the park — the Petit Grepon. The Petit is situated in a dramatic group of gendarmes in the Sky Pond Basin. The approach is beautiful, though the trail to Loch Vale is crowded during midday hours. One of the best laughs I've ever had was on a trail run with my friend Karl. We passed a cluttered group of tourists, likely of the Middle America variety, who seemed confused as to why anyone would be running on a trail at a high elevation. Karl noticed their confused stares, and with a believable primal scream, yelled, "BEAR!"

A tower climber at heart, I have thoroughly enjoyed both Zowie and the Petit Grepon. Despite the Grepon's fame, I think Zowie is a more beautiful climb, devoid of a tedious descent, and graced with a spectacular approach. (Steve "Crusher" Bartlett, who proof read this guidebook, disagrees with this statement. So there you have it — two different opinions). I suppose you'll need to do both!

Petit Grepon
& Penknife
photo:
Gary
Neptune

Petit Grepon

Approach the Petit Grepon via the Glacier Gorge trailhead; follow the Loch Vale trail at the juncture, but continue beyond the Loch on a more primitive trail to Sky Pond. From Sky Pond, the Petit is obvious to the north.

Begin **South Face** (III, 5.8) on the North Face in an unprotected difficult finger crack— just kidding. The route begins, as the name suggests, on the South Face, and ascends the prominent chimney system past a large terrace to an even larger terrace, near the tower's midpoint. The chimney is gained from the ground by scampering up easy slabs. The long first pitch is about 5.6. An easier second pitch continues up the obvious chimney until a belay is possible. Continue up the chimney/crack (5.6) until one reaches the upper terrace.

The first pitch above the terrace continues up a chimney to a slanting wide crack (5.7). Step left at a good ledge and belay.

The next pitch follows the crack system then angles right. At a large roof, traverse right to an optional belay stance where the overhang ends, or continue up a 5.8 corner to a ledge near the SE arete and belay there.

The next long pitch is where the spectacular and exposed climbing begins. Wander up corners to the right of the main face and ends up at a stance on the arete.

Another lead (5.7+) climbs a crack and then wanders, once again, up the east side of the formation to a ledge beneath the final summit pitch.

A short lead attains the shelf then continues up the spectacular summit ridge to the top. Descend by rappeling 50 meters into the notch; or make two shorter rappels which I do not recommend, as this involves interacting with a talus-covered ledge. Next, scramble north up the gully and ascend a short 5.4 chimney. Now descend northwards into the Gash, staying mostly leftish when the path cliffs out. Eventually one reaches the Andrews Glacier Trail— a beautiful path through the alpine meadows beneath Mt. Otis.

This standard descent offers a wonderful round-trip outing, but requires climbing with all of one's equipment. To return to Sky Pond, resist the temptation to rappel the nasty gullies on the sides of the spire. Instead, when one reaches terra firma above the easy chimney, traverse east behind the Saber and Cathedral Spires to a saddle that is obvious from Sky Pond. Head down this gully which broadens dramatically. Follow a path of least resistance, heading left (or east) when difficulties are encountered. Take the left fork above and left of a small spire in the gully and follow this path until the descent seemingly cliffs out. Though a rappel station on some slabs may be tempting, it is better to head to the east and look for a chimney downclimb. The ten foot chimney seems improbable at first but isn't too bad. From this point it's just a walk through the boulders back to the pond.

A recent bolted rappel route has also been added to the Petit. No doubt this will further increase traffic as it decreases commitment

Penknife

The Pen Knife (I 5.6) No one in their right mind would hike in, scramble to the base, and climb this tower for its own sake, but if you've just sent the Petit and have time to spare... The route climbs the northeast ridge of the little spire north of the Petit, with the difficulties easing as one goes higher. The descent involves much downclimbing.

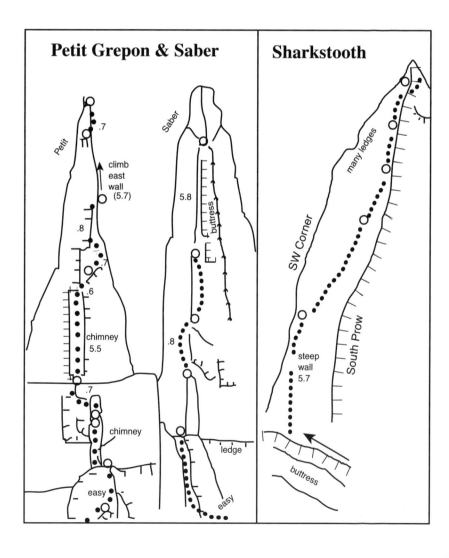

Petit Grepon & Saber

Petit

.7

climb
east
wall
(5.7)

.8

.7

.6

chimney
5.5

.7

chimney

easy

Saber

5.8

buttress

.8

ledge

easy

Sharkstooth

many ledges

SW Corner

South Prow

steep
wall
5.7

buttress

Sharkstooth

The Sharkstooth is west of the Petit, and will probably be the only Cathedral summit you can find on a map. Hike to Sky Pond, then continue west of the Petit up a grueling talus slope/gully affair. Pass below a small buttress on the left, then head right above the buttress and begin on the SW corner of the formation.

South Prow (5.7) starts up the west wall. Run out the rope over 5.7 rock to a nice big belay ledge to the left of the broad southern arete. Belay.

The second pitch heads out right, then straight up to a very large belay ledge.

Two or three more pitches of 5.7 head right up the prow. Stay on the prow itself for the best rock. Once you reach a point directly below the final headwall, head right to the East Bowl (an obvious bowl under the summit). Pick a line to the top (maximum 5.6).

Descend by rappeling the **East Gully** route via fixed anchors. The first anchors lie a little below the summit just above a vertical dihedral. This descent puts one back at the East Col. Descend from here via the standard gash walkout.

Saber

The Saber is the spire directly east of the Petit. Approach the same as for the South Face of the Petit.

Southeast Corner (5.9) Begin at the SE corner of the low angle slabs and scramble up 300' to gain a big ledge. Walk to the left along the ledge and climb a thin crack (crux) up the right side of the west face. Belay on a nice ledge.

Head straight up for two more pitches on the prow that divides the west face from the south face, aiming for the large left facing dihedral that dominates the upper south face. The first of these two pitches stays to the right following shallow corners. Where these peter out, belay. The next pitch heads back left via face climbing. Belay below the corner.

Climb the astonishing corner for two pitches (5.8) and belay on a ledge beneath the easy ridge to the summit.

Climb the ridge for two pitches to the summit.

Descend as for the Petit Grepon by either continuing down the Gash or returning via the large gully.

Zowie

The resemblance of this granite spire to the Petit Grepon had apparently caused some parties to ascend this route instead of its more famous twin. This mix-up should be easy to prevent as the approach is altogether different. Zowie isn't an official member of the Cathedral Spires, but it's just as great. Zowie is, in fact, part of Mount Otis, so if you're looking at a map....

The approach begins the same as for the Petit, but once the far side of The Loch is reached, take the rightmost trail to Andrews Glacier, rather than the left trail to Sky Pond. From here, hike a little over a mile and Zowie becomes obvious on the south flanks of Mt. Otis; hike directly to its base to the start of the route.

In my opinion, **South Face** (III, 5.8) is the best route of its grade in RMNP's high country. Similar to the Grepon in difficulty, it offers one of the most beautiful descents coupled with an outrageously exposed crux pitch. (The average 5.8 leader will find this a sandbag being stumped on the badly unprotected offwidth.)

The route begins just left of a huge chimney but eventually moves into it, terminating at the large terrace.

A 250 foot walk along this terrace leads to a belay at the SE edge of the spire. From here, many 5.6-5.7 possibilities exist for the next two pitches. The further right you stay, generally speaking, the easier the climbing is. Essentially, one winds up on a ledge beneath the final summit block and the crux pitch of the tower.

A short traverse left takes you to a squeeze chimney formed by a detached flake on the tower's left side. Ascend this very exposed and scarcely protected pitch.

Descend by rappelling from the summit until one reaches bizarre vertically hanging meadows interspersed with short cliff sections. A combination of scrambles and rappels takes you down the western gully system. Much of this gully is filled with beautiful wild flowers.

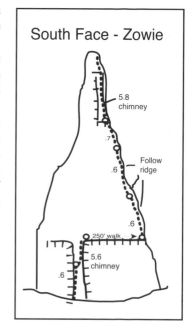

South Face - Zowie

5.8 chimney

.7

.6

Follow ridge

.6

250' walk

5.6 chimney

.6

Hallett Peak

The North Face of Hallett Peak is one of the most striking walls in Rocky Mountain National Park; the approach is quite short and scenic; the route finding, however, is a bitch.

The North Face of Hallett, if one steps away from it, can be viewed as three distinct buttresses. No one climbs on the first (easternmost) buttress. The second buttress is probably the most popular as it houses several excellent routes, crammed near each other on its eastern side. The third (furthest west) buttress contains (what I am told is the classic) the **Northcutt-Carter**. On two occasions I have started up this route and failed to follow it for its duration. Both times, I summited Halletts but wound up significantly right of where I started. I haven't been back in about eight years, so my route descriptions are based on those of less Hallett-dyslexic friends with more recent and successful experience on the route.

Approach: Drive to the Bear Lake parking lot and hike to Emerald Lake. At the lake, head to the left through the talus, aiming for the top of the moraine. Stay high on this shelf and a trail through the talus becomes obvious.

Descent: My descent description assumes that all parties will hike to the west, since they are certainly aiming for the actual summit. A large gully drops to the west behind the third buttress. Scramble down into the gully, and where it is possible to cross easily to the most western (or leftmost gully as one is looking down), do so. A scramble down scree on a pronounced path takes one to a spot where the trail splits. Again, go west (leftward), to the ground. Rappel slings are a sign that you are off route; if you encounter rap stations, explore alternative descents.

The Love Route (III, 5.9) is pretty fun, though it does sport some wandering loose pitches. A big loose buttress forms a big loose dihedral on the big loose left side of the second buttress. Climb in or near this dihedral for three easy (5.4) pitches (occasional fixed gear reminds the climber that she is on route). The third pitch ends on a ledge about thirty feet above the pillar (one bolt at the belay).

A spectacular 5.7 pitch ascends the exposed wall via discontinuous cracks and beautiful face climbing. Several belay ledges exist, but try to find one fairly high up, so the next pitch is not too much of a rope-stretcher.

A wandering slabular 5.7 pitch takes one to a belay on a slab in an overhanging grassy cubby hole.

The next pitch climbs out the ugly overhang past oodles of antiquated fixed pitons (9+) and continues to a belay atop the slab (163 feet). A very short scramble takes one to the summit talus. Remember not to fall on Love.

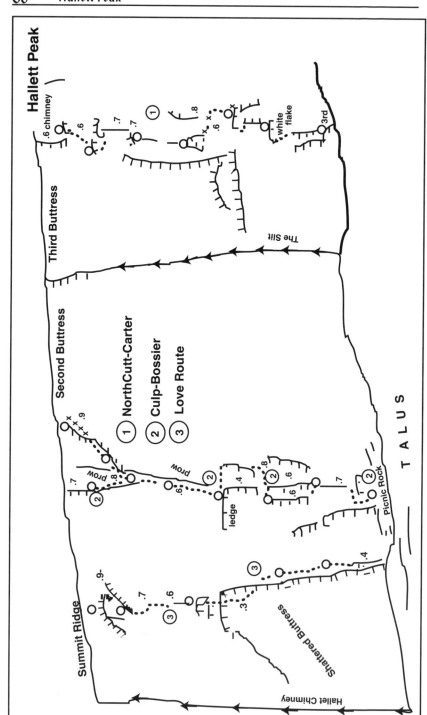

Culp-Bossier (III, 5.8+) is the best route on Hallett, but suffers from the normal problem of the vast route-finding possibilities. One can climb almost anywhere in the vicinity of the route without great difficulties, but also without great protection. Begin at a pink band of rock in the prominent dihedral right of the Love Route. At an obvious ledge traverse right to a 5.7 finger crack which gains a belay stance (140').

Climb a right-facing dihedral until it's easy to climb up and left into another right-facing dihedral (5.5). This pitch ends at a stance about 100' up.

Follow the dihedral to the right past some fixed pins. Pull a roof and follow another dihedral to a belay stance (5.8, 155').

Short corners lead to a belay in the large band of white rock (5.5, 80')

A wild and exposed pitch begins in a shallow corner and climbs the wall left of the obvious prow (5.7). Belay at the start of a shallow dihedral (145').

Another fine pitch wanders above this one to a belay on a ramp (5.7, 120'). Both pitches offer sporadic protection. [One can also climb directly up the exposed and unprotected prow for two full pitches –truly spectacular and the line taken on the first ascent– instead of climbing the 2 pitches just described.]

The next pitch climbs the steep groove/crack left of a right-facing dihedral. Pass a roof (5.8), head right and cruise a full rope length to a belay site.

Traverse beneath the roof passing a bolt, then back left to a corner (5.8, 100'). Scramble to the summit.

Northcutt-Carter (III, 5.7) is another of the three climbs included in 50 Classic Climbs of North America. It is a busy line, but route-finding difficulty often restricts activity to the first pitch.

Begin on the left side of the Third Buttress below two big dihedrals. Scramble up to the dihedrals, pick the right one and climb to a slot. Head left via face climbing, then ascend a white flake (5.5, 120'). Belay on a nice ledge.

Ascend a left facing corner for about 10 feet. Do not continue up this corner; instead, traverse left into a white open-book which turns into a right-angling flake crack. Hand traverse right to a good ledge and belay. (5.6, 150')

The third pitch heads up for a bit, then breaks out left and up past two pins, heading for a pillar above. Climb the right side of the pillar and belay on top (5.6, 150').

Head straight up cracks that change from a shallow right-facing dihedral to a left-facing dihedral (5.5). Belay below a roof in an alcove after 140'.

Turn the roof on the right, then ascend a crack (crux) until it ends. Where it does, head left to vegetated ledge and belay (5.7, 160').

The sixth pitch heads right slightly and moves over 5.6 face to a belay on another ledge beneath a roof (160').

The final pitch climbs up into a 5.6 chimney above the roof and continues to the top of the wall.

Notchtop

Notchtop is another of the park's worthy objectives. The east face rivals Hallett's in vertical size and the climbing is every bit as spectacular.

Approach Notchtop from the Bear Lake parking lot. Follow signs to Lake Helene. Walk around the lake on its northwest shore, then pick up a path which leads up past Grace Falls to a bench. From here, scramble up the talus to the base.

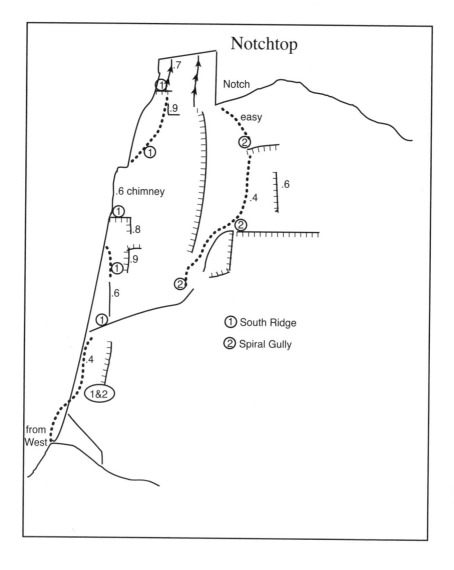

Notchtop

① South Ridge
② Spiral Gully

Descend from the top of Notch Spire (please rope up) by downclimbing the broken terrain to reach the "notch." From here scramble along the east side of the ridge and gain the true summit of Notchtop. An exposed ramp along the west side of the peak leads to a fairly easy gully. Follow exposed ledges along the west face for 200+ feet to a saddle. From the saddle, pick up a much easier gully down the west side to the base. Many people don't traverse far enough and decide to rappel a steep gully near the notch. The first rappel looks gripping, so look around for the proper descent.

South Ridge (5.9) ascends the prominent ridge on the left side of the east face all the way to the top. Many variations to this route exist and as such routefinding can be difficult. Begin in the descent gully below a ramp which heads to the south buttress. Ascend the easy (5.4) buttress for two pitches and belay on a big grassy ledge. These pitches are the same as for **Spiral Gully**.

From the left side (lower side) of the ledge, face climb up and left to a good belay ledge (5.6, 75').

Head left over to the arete and continue up a flake on the west face to a small ledge on the west side (5.7+, 150').

Climb the dihedral above, then head right at its top, cross the prow, and belay on another ledge (5.7, 85').

Ascend the chimney to the left and belay on a ledge at its end (5.6, 100').

Face climb up and slightly right, aiming for the left edge of the roof/bulge above. Climb the crack past the left side of the roof (crux) and belay on yet another ledge.

Climb the groove to the summit.

Spiral Gully (5.4) is a super moderate route that winds all the way around the east face and summits in the notch.

Begin in the descent gully and climb up to the ramp as described in **South Ridge**. Belay.

Traverse the ramp to the right. Where it ends climb up 5.4 rock to a big grassy area called the East Meadows. Belay.

Ascend the terrain below the notch for two more pitches. The easiest climbing lies on the left side of the terrain below the notch. Better rock exists right of here, but the climbing is more in the 5.6-5.7 range

Jules Raymond on the
South Ridge of Notchtop.
Photo by Fred Knapp

LONGS PEAK AREA

The Longs Peak Region of Rocky Mountain National Park is home to its namesake, the highest peak within the park. The spectacular east face of Longs Peak houses the Diamond, one of the world's greatest alpine walls. Most of the climbing in this region is contained within the spectacular cirque formed by Mt. Meeker, Longs Peak, and Mt. Lady Washington.

The Longs Peak Ranger Station & Campground is located 8.5 miles south of Estes Park on Highway 7. A recently paved, well-labeled road leads to the parking area, restrooms, Ranger Station, and trailhead. The parking lot is often completely filled by 5:00am on summer weekends, as the hike to Long's summit is one of the most popular nontechnical alpine adventures in the park.

The trail begins just behind the bathroom and Visitor's Center and is clearly marked and labeled. Once the Diamond comes into view, the trail splits at a juncture near horse corrals and bathrooms. The left-hand fork takes one to Chasm Lake and the base of Mt. Meeker's Flying Buttress. The right hand fork climbs to the Boulderfield, the Cables Route, and the Keyhole (the third class route). This latter path is used if one is rappelling from Chasm View to Broadway (the big ledge which cuts across the base of the Diamond). For all other approaches—the North Chimney, Chasm View Wall routes, and the **Flying Buttress**—the Chasm Lake Trail is the approach.

Bruce Miller enjoying a snowy birthday on the Diamond's Table Ledge
photo: Fred Knapp

Mount Meeker (13,911)

On the approach route, when the Chasm Lake Cirque first comes into view, a very prominent rib forms a striking feature on Mt. Meeker's North Face. This is the **Flying Buttress**, an excellent 5.9 route.

Hike the Chasm Lake trail to the roofless outhouses in the meadow near the Chasm Lake Shelter. Follow a trail and primitive path to the snowfields at the base of Meeker.

The Flying Buttress (III, 5.9) when viewed straight-on is one of the most striking lines in the Park. An abundance of climbable lines, however, makes finding the 5.9 route somewhat tricky. Most parties encounter some 5.10 terrain as they veer from the original line. The route begins in a dihedral on the left side of the buttress. Step right into a V-shaped chimney and then continue up a slab for a 150' pitch ending on a ledge. (Many people follow the hand cracks on the prow until they turn into thin 5.10c cracks about 120' up).

From the belay ledge, the easiest route ascends a dihedral on the east side of the rib and arrives at a long belay ledge with 2 bolts. (5.9, 150'). It is also possible to arrive at this point by staying on the rib proper following thin 5.10 cracks which turn to 5.8 hands.

From here, a prominent corner system flows along the right side of the face. Fixed pins abound and it is possible to climb a variety of lines on either side of the prow for about two pitches. The easiest route involves moving left from the bolts, following a finger crack until it is possible to step left to a left-facing dihedral. About 15' beneath a roof traverse right past a bolt and pass the right side of the roof past two pins. Now, step back onto the main face and run the rope out to a long ledge.

Two more pitches take one up ramp systems to the top of the prow (some short steep headwalls provide the cruxes).

Descend from here by scrambling down the gully to the right (west) or continue via fifth class slabs and scrambling to Meeker's summit (still a ways away) and descend the Loft via a series of ledges and gullies formed by the juncture of Meeker and Longs.

Gary Neptune photo

Longs Peak

This is the big boy. The East Face of Longs contains the most stellar long routes in Colorado. The very altitude adds difficulty and the lack of sunlight provides a real mountain experience. (Routes on the Diamond start at 13,000 and many climb shaded right-facing dihedrals, even when the few hours of sun shine on the wall). Descend from the summit via a cairn-marked path down the north face and rappel from the old cable route eyebolts just above the lone steep section. From here one can hike down via the boulderfield trail or return to Mills Glacier by descending "the Camel" gully. The latter is a gully system between Chasm View Wall and Mt. Lady Washington. Delicate scrambling takes one to a wide grassy ledge which runs west along Chasm View Wall; walking along this is much easier than continuing down the Camel gully. Scope it out from the base before you do your route. For those who aren't interested in summitting Longs, a rappel route exists down D7. From "Almost Table Ledge" the route is bolted with camouflaged hangers and is somewhat difficult to find as it doesn't take a perfect plum line. Rappel slowly and look for bolted stations. Most raps are between 150-160' between stations. If you're not at bolts, you're off route. Rappels for the North Chimney begin at bolts near the bottom of slabs on Broadway. Again, the proper rappel stations are bolted with modern 3/8" bolts.

Lower East Face

While the Diamond is the most popular objective on Longs, two other great routes ascend the Lower East Face: **Stettner's Ledges** and **Kiener's** (or Mountaineer's Route).

Stettner's Ledges (5.7+) was a groundbreaking route in its day (first ascent in 1927, and is now one of the all-time classics on Longs' flanks. The route climbs the lower east face below the Diamond, ending on Broadway. This poses a dilemma, for there is no easy way down from the top of **Stettner's**. The choices are to either follow **Kiener's** to the summit (a good option if the weather is holding) or traverse Broadway to Lamb's Slide (the 45 degree snowfield that lies to the left of the east face). From here, cross the ice field and descend the rock rib on the far side back to the base.

Approach **Stettner's** by hiking up to Chasm Lake and circumnavigating it on the right side. Hike up the talus towards Mills Glacier (the permanent snowfield which lies below the east face), heading left towards the convergence of Lamb's Slide and the talus. Look for a snow tongue on the upper left edge which leads to the base of the rock. The route starts here. Climb up into the very long right facing corner which leans left. The next corner to the right is **Striped Wall**. Don't start up this, as a spot of A4 exists right off the deck. Ascend the corner for two pitches, each about 130 feet in length. The second belay stance is in an alcove.

The third pitch heads out the right side of the alcove and climbs past several pitons (this is the famed "piton ladder"). Continue up the corner until it turns into a good belay spot at Lunch Ledge (a large ledge with loose blocks, 5.7+, 140').

Walk to the left side of the ledge and climb a vertical 5.6 corner. Belay on another ledge.

Now head left into the Yellow Bowl (5.5 terrain) for two more pitches, ending on Broadway. A better finish from the ledge at the end of the fourth pitch ascends the right facing corner system straight up for two more pitches to Broadway. This finish is called **Hornsby Direct** (5.8).

Kiener's (5.3) was the first winter ascent of the east face, and the subsequent descent claimed the life of Agnes Vaille, a prominent member of the Colorado Mountain Club. A memorial shelter to her now exists at the Keyhole on the hiking route to the summit.

The route starts at the base of Lamb's Slide. Either climb the Slide itself (crampons and ice axe required, especially in late season), or ascend the rib to the left of the Slide. Traverse onto Broadway when level with it. This entails crossing Lamb's Slide if the rib was climbed.

Now traverse about 1000 feet to the base of the Notch Couloir, the gully left of the Diamond which leads up to the Notch. This is hairball traversing over low fifth class terrain. The exposure is mind blowing...rope up for this. On the right side of the couloir is a nice belay stance at two bolts.

From here, head left into the Notch, climb up for 30-40 feet, cut right and climb up a bunch of small step-like features (5.3). Belay at a couple of pitons in the chimney.

Finish climbing the chimney, head right at its top into a narrow section. Squirm out onto a ledge and belay on the right side.

Cut left and up over strange little steps and short dihedrals. This is a very long pitch and entails probably 5.0 climbing. Another pitch, this one only 60 feet, ends on top of the dihedrals.

Scramble up almost 800 feet of talus, always heading right. Two pitches climb up "The Staircase", a stretch of large boulder steps. At its end, head right,very close to the edge of the Diamond. Don't climb up into the massive dihedral at the top of the Diamond! Once above the top of the Diamond and right of the huge corner, look for cairns marking the way onto the north slopes; and the summit. Descend the North Face as described on page 85.

EAST FACE OF LONGS PEAK

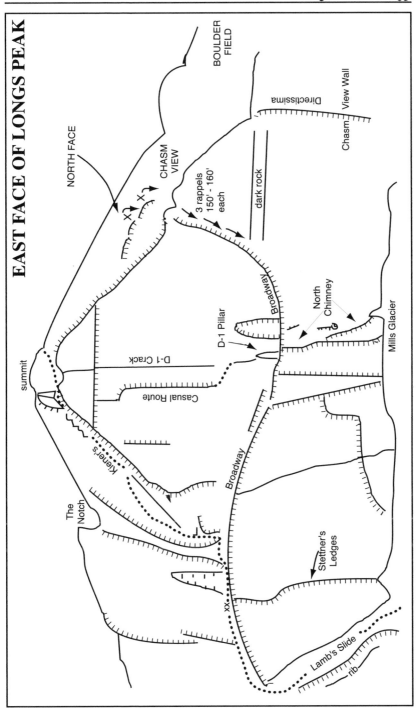

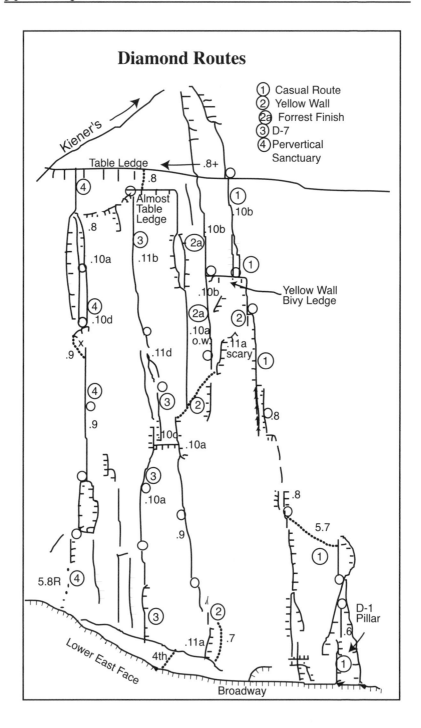

Diamond Routes

① Casual Route
② Yellow Wall
②a Forrest Finish
③ D-7
④ Pervertical Sanctuary

Kiener's

Table Ledge   .8+

④   .8

Almost Table Ledge

① 10b

.8

③   10b

.10a   ②a

.11b

④   .10b

.10d   ②a   ②

x   .10a
.9   o.w

Yellow Wall Bivy Ledge

.11a scary

.11d   ①

④   ③   ②

.9   .8

.10c   .10a

③   .10a

.10a   ③

.9

④   ②

5.8R   ③   .7

5.7   ①

D-1 Pillar

.8

.6

.11a
4th   ②   ①

Lower East Face

Broadway

The Diamond

The most famous wall in the park and the crowning jewel on any park climber's resume. Need we say more? The Diamond is probably the most renowned alpine wall in the U.S., and with a nice range of routes to choose from it should head the objective list of anyone who climbs solid 5.10 and up.

Be sure to start very early (most parties shoot to be at the base of the North Chimney and ready to climb by sunrise) due to the double factors of storms and sunlight. The sun leaves the Diamond around noon, and at 14,000 feet things get a bit chilly.

Access to the Diamond is most frequently gained via a somewhat miserable affair called the North Chimney. This is the prominent feature just right of center on the lower east face. Hike around Chasm Lake on the right (north) side, trudge up the talus slope, and gain Mills Glacier (the permanent snowfield below the face). Bring a rock to chop steps in Mills, especially late in the season when it becomes hard glazed ice. Climb up the snow tongue into the chimney. The best route up the chimney begins left of the longest tongue and climbs slabs and dihedrals up to a chockstone. Step left, pass the chockstone, then head right into a left facing dihedral. Head up and left over slabs, then back right to an easy crack (5.5). Where it ends, find an easy ramp which heads left and up and puts one on Broadway (wide ledge beneath The Diamond proper). Traverse left on Broadway and head to the base of your route. **Warning:** Several climbers have been the victims of tragedy or near-tragedy when they became complacent on Broadway and unroped for the traverse. The ledge is often wet and is quite narrow in spots. Please be careful.

1. The Casual Route

The Casual Route (IV, 5.10b) is the most popular route on the Diamond and thus has earned such nicknames as the "Cattle Route" and the "Casualty Route", the latter name stemming from the number of inexperienced climbers lured by the relatively easy grade.

The route begins about 100 feet left of North Chimney at the base of the D-1 Pillar. Climb the middle of the prominent pillar starting via a left facing corner followed by face holds above (5.5). Set up anchors and belay at a good stance.

Next, climb the left side of the pillar and belay below a 5.9 finger crack.

Climb the crack, and look for a piton near a shelf to the left. This marks the start of the traverse. Now a rising traverse left across large holds (5.7) can be made. This traverse gains a right facing corner at its end. The traverse is protected by fixed pitons; don't make the mistake of traversing too low, as this is much harder. Look for the pins. Belay in slings at the base of the large right facing corner at the end of the traverse.

Ascend the 5.8 corner and belay at a good ledge.

Another short 5.8 pitch takes one up another right facing corner.

And yet another 5.8 corner takes one to the huge "Yellow Wall Bivy Ledge".

Now the crux begins up a cold and often wet squeeze chimney that exits into the crux crack. The 10b move occurs at a bulge protected by a pin. Stepping slightly right at the pin makes this section a tad easier.

Traverse left for about two pitches along Table Ledge (the ledge that cuts across the upper part of the Diamond). There is a spot of 5.8 here, but that ends the difficulties. At the end of Table Ledge, join **Kiener's** which follows the stair steps of boulders to the summit of Longs (or rappel D7) ; careful route finding (see **Kiener's** description) keeps this as third class.

2. The Yellow Wall

The **Yellow Wall** (IV, 5.10d R) is one of the Diamond's finer routes and is often busy on weekends.

Begin left of **Casual Route** and left of a nice bivy cave at a left facing corner with two fixed pins. The corner is 5.11a, but the difficulties can be avoided by ascending the face just right of the arete (formed by the dihedral's right wall). If taking this 5.8 alternative, one can still clip the uppermost pin, but the climbing is unprotected to this point. Belay at a stance.

The next pitch climbs a good 5.9 crack pitch with supplemental edges (120 feet).

Backstroke your way up the notoriously wet shallow corner of the third pitch until it is possible to move left to a drier crack which gains a ledge with bolts.

The **Yellow Wall** proper traverses right for about 20 feet, wandering past cracks and dihedrals until it gains the notorious **Yellow Wall** traverse. Belay in slings at a small stance.

The next pitch is noted for its collection of tired rurps, bashies, and RPs. This traverse is about 10c and leads one to a short difficult dihedral. The only pro in this shallow left facing corner is an old piton, so don't fall (10d). This pitch can be continued to gain the Yellow Wall Bivy Ledge (involves about 10 feet of simul-climbing) or one can belay on another reasonable ledge.

Finish the route via the crux pitch on **Casual Route**, and exit off Table Ledge.

Forrest Finish variation: from the sloping ledge atop the third pitch, one can ascend the first crack system to the right (the system directly above the sling belay at the start of the Yellow Wall Traverse) for two long pitches to Table Ledge. Both pitches are excellent 5.10b.

3. D7

Many consider **D7** (V 5.11d) to be the finest route on the Diamond. This route begins about 150 feet left of the bivy cave.

Climb the broken rock above Broadway to a ledge beneath a left facing corner (5.4, 40 feet, often scrambled). Continue up the corner for 70 feet, ignore the belay ledge, and continue up the crack on the right (5.9, long pitch).

A 100 foot pitch begins up a left facing corner and ends at a ledge.

Another 100 foot pitch climbs the wide 5.10 crack to the belay shared with **Yellow Wall**.

Climb the rightmost of the two corners (right facing) for about 100 feet to a sloping belay.

Continue up the corner/crack system (crux) for a long pitch ending on a ledge to the left.

A 5.11a pitch continues up the crack to Table Ledge.

D7 has many fixed pins, and therefore devours quickdraws - bring at least 15 and a modest selection of nuts and Friends.

4. Pervertical Sanctuary

Pervertical Sanctuary (IV, 5.10d) was originally a grade VI aid route that started on the Lower East Face, but today most people climb only the Diamond pitches.

The route starts left of a bolt ladder (left of D-7) and climbs over 5.8 runout terrain to the base of The Mitten, an obvious flake on the far left side of the Diamond. Belay below The Mitten.

Climb the left side of The Mitten and belay at its top (5.8).

A 5.9 pitch climbs the crack directly above. Belay at a cozy stance.

Another 5.9 pitch leaves the comfy belay for the good corner which ends at a short face section (protected by an old bent bolt). Belay at a good stance.

Gain a thin 5.10 crack on the right which slowly widens to fists after 150' (5.10d-crux); the thin crack to the left is **Ariana** (a two pitch variation - 5.12a & 5.11 respectfully). The right crack is 5.10. Follow it to a belay at a wedged flake.

The next long pitch (10a) ascends a crack to a belay at a long ledge - "Almost Table Ledge".

A final pitch heads up a 5.9 dihedral to Table Ledge. Bring a double set of Friends for this route.

Chasm View Wall

Chasm View Wall, while not as spectacular as the Diamond, is home to several excellent routes. The climbs are consistently steep and as long as the routes on the Diamond that climb from Broadway to Table ledge, yet they do not require the approach to Broadway, the involved descent, or the commitment of the Diamond. Also, Chasm View Wall sees sun all day, making for good high altitude tanning.

Approach Chasm View Wall by hiking to the lake and skirting it on the north side. Hike up to Mills Glacier, then head back right along a tricky ledge and ramp system to the base of the routes. You can bivy at Chasm View Boulderfield with a permit.

Descend from Chasm View Wall routes via the Camel gully (see Longs Peak introduction section).

1. Red Wall

Red Wall (III, 5.10) is a deceptively time consuming outing, and the grade III rating may not be entirely fair.

The route begins with easy fifth class climbing up the center of the wall. The goal is to gain a ramp which angles up from left to right. Climb the dihedral in the back of the ramp (5.7) to a belay at a large sloping shelf.

The next pitch climbs the difficult corner (10c). An easier variation involves a traverse down and left to where it is possible to climb a right facing corner to the same stance (5.8).

One might wish to move the belay further along the ledge to a point underneath a system of hollow flakes. Climb through these flakes to a cramped belay at an old bolt and a pin.

The next pitch ascends a right facing corner system, gained by a short traverse to the right. The crux occurs at a traverse beneath a large roof (10b/c). Belay just above the roof.

A very long 5.9 pitch continues up corners to a point where the crack gets very thin and steep. At this point, one can step right across the sloping ledge (past a bolt) and enter a 5.8 chimney, or one can climb straight up the tricky thin crack (5.9). Both end at a ledge beneath an alcove.

A long traverse right takes one to an obvious exit to the top of the wall (5.7, 150 feet).

2. Directissima

Directissima (III, 5.10) is the better of the two classic routes as it takes a straight line through the wall's center (thus the name). The route ascends the right facing corner system up the middle of the wall.

Easy fifth class and scrambling up the ramps gains the crack system. The first pitch is a 5.9 and ends at a good ledge.

Fred researching on
the Red Wall
Bruce Miller photo

The second pitch can follow the right hand crack at 5.10, or the left corner at 5.9. Either way, they join at a belay beneath overhanging flakes.

A 5.9+ offwidth pitch tackles the section above, protected by two old bolts. The next pitch continues up the corner and provides some of the best crack climbing in the park (5.10). A short finishing pitch deposits you on top.

Descend via the Camel gully described in the Longs Peak introduction.

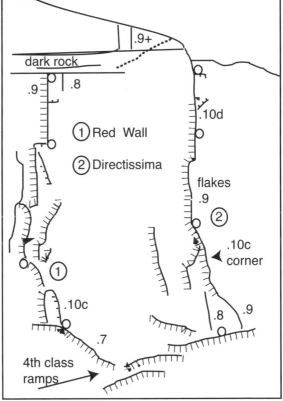

.9+

dark rock

.9   .8

① Red Wall

② Directissima

.10d

flakes
.9   ②

.10c
corner

①

.10c

.7

.8   .9

4th class
ramps

Route Index